Through My Own Eyes

THROUGH
An Awakened

Theodore Isaac Rubin, M.D.

MY OWN EYES
Unconscious

MACMILLAN PUBLISHING CO., INC.
NEW YORK

Copyright © 1982 by Theodore Isaac Rubin, M.D.

Macmillan Publishing Co., Inc.
866 Third Avenue, New York, N.Y. 10022
Collier Macmillan Canada, Inc.

Library of Congress Cataloging in Publication Data

Rubin, Theodore Isaac.
    Through my own eyes.

    1. Rubin, Theodore Isaac.   2. Psychiatrists—
United States—Biography.   3. Subconsciousness.
I. Title.
RC339.52.R8A38   616.89'0092'4 [B]   81-20692
ISBN 0-02-605700-X   AACR2

10   9   8   7   6   5   4   3   2   1

Printed in the United States of America

To Ellie, my Mrs. Sotto these many years, and the picnics you made those evenings on the beach at Truro.

Also by Theodore Isaac Rubin:

Jordi
Lisa and David
In the Life
Sweet Daddy
Cat
Platzo and the Mexican Pony Rider
The 29th Summer
Coming Out
The Thin Book by a Formerly Fat Psychiatrist
The Winner's Notebook
Emergency Room Diary
The Angry Book
Dr. Rubin, Please Make Me Happy
Compassion and Self Hate
Understanding Your Man
Shrink
Love Me Love My Fool
Forever Thin
Reflections in a Goldfish Tank
Alive and Fat and Thinning in America
Reconciliations

I'll Always Love Georgy Sotto's Mother: A Zen Interlude

I WENT over to Georgy Sotto's house that Saturday morning hoping that his mother would give us some smoked eel. She did and we laughed. God, how we could laugh. Sometimes we would laugh and eat through a whole morning and I'd leave feeling full and happy, the muscles of my belly aching and hard with food and from laughing.

Georgy's house was really five houses. Mr. Sotto had found the five empty houses over twenty or more years and he slowly put them all together on the beach. Two stretched out lengthwise and three were bunched on top, overlapping the bottom two. There were doors, porches, kitchens, and bathrooms in the most unexpected places, and there were at least thirty-five rooms. The whole thing was six stories high. I used to stay over fairly often, sometimes for weeks at a time. I had my own room which Georgy's mother never gave to anyone else, even though there were times I didn't show up for several months. My room was on top and was fairly big. The windows opposite the doorway faced the bay. I could see the ocean and beach for miles and miles. It was the neatest, cleanest house I've ever seen, and yet I can't remember ever seeing Georgy's mother cleaning. Maybe this is the way with Japanese people, keeping it all sparse and neat, but very warm and gentle and beautiful too, just like Georgy's mother. This was the way she looked, her long black hair, her half shell eyelashes, her skin, her smile, and more than anything, the way she moved. Her hands and head and the way she walked were as gentle as peaceful and soft as anything I've ever seen. Georgy and I were fifteen years old, and his mother must have been thirty-five or so. Mr. Sotto was much older.

The house was a kind of rooming house for the Japanese

people who worked in the various restaurants and small businesses on the island. Yet it wasn't a rooming house at all. It was a home to them, a real home, and they could stay there as long as they wanted. It wasn't just single Japanese men who lived there; there were also a few women, and sometimes whole families stayed there for several months until they got their own place to live. Some of them gave Georgy's mother money, but mostly they brought her food and other odd things like furniture, clothes, and things. There were rooming houses on the island, and for a while my family lived in one. They were cold, dirty places with no central heart, nothing like Georgy's house, but just rooms off halls.

Mr. Sotto spent most of his time fixing and adding to the house. He was the carpenter, plumber, and painter. He also spent time on the beach walking and "listening and looking." He never fished with us and always thanked us over and over again for any fish the rest of us brought to the house. Mr. Sotto was considered a very wise man, and at one time or another nearly every Japanese on the island consulted him. Even Rikko, the richest man around, came to him. These "consultations" were never secret: they took place whenever the man in need came to the house, and anyone around stayed on and listened too. Mostly this is what Mr. Sotto did —listen. He'd say very little, a few words here and there, and the man, no matter how agitated he seemed when he came in, would go out at peace. I never heard Mr. Sotto give direct advice, not once.

Looking back now, I guess Georgy's mother gave everyone a sweet warm feel of the world through herself and the house, and being with his father made a person feel his own peaceful ways and self. I used to go there whenever the world felt cold and when the feel of me got weak and shaky and noisy. I'd look at Georgy's mother, stay in the house a few days, talk to Mr. Sotto, and I'd feel quiet and warm with myself again.

After we ate that Saturday, the four of us went into the big middle room and sat around on straw mats and drank tea. After a while Rikko came in and spoke to Mr. Sotto. He said that he was depressed and couldn't understand the reason for it.

"Business is good. I'm healthy. I'm strong. My sons are away in good schools and are doing well. My wife is fine. What can it be? I wake in the morning and I feel clouded inside. A weight sits on my chest. Nothing makes me happy. We have a nice house. I sit in my garden and I have no peace. A small animal sits in my chest and eats away. I've even thought of suicide. Why?"

We sat silently. Rikko drank tea too. He seemed calm now. Then Mr. Sotto spoke.

"When I was your age, forty-five or so, I finally arrived at that point where I knew that what I had thought I was missing in life didn't really exist. Dreams about vacuums and infinite space occurred at the same time. I would wake up, unsure as to whether I was dreaming of death or, worse yet, of life.

"I forced myself to look inward and I'd see storming seas, mountains, terrible fires, earthquakes, faces screaming, and light blue quiet skies and eagles soaring and swooping down on rabbits, and vast stretches of beaches and deserts and raging snowstorms and icy glaciers and faces—many faces caught in endlessness, trapped in forever. And there in the middle of it all I found a small walled garden with stones and a brook and tiny birds, and again and again when I felt my worst I'd go to that garden—through the storms and faces—and I'd rest and eventually the heavy feel of myself left and the dreams of vacuums stopped."

Rikko shook his hand and left.

.   .   .

I HATED GREY DAYS and yearned for the sun, but my yearning changed nothing. There were many times when the greyness hung on for weeks and we'd get fog or rain or both without letup. I used to get some relief in Rikko's restaurant, first because he kept it well lighted and there were always a lot of people there. But there was more to it than that.

Rikko's restaurant was actually a single huge circular room on the beach. The kitchen took up the entire periphery of the room, and the much larger inner circle consisted of many different sized tables and chairs. Rikko had a reputation for never refusing to give a man a job, therefore there were always a great many cooks, dish-washers, and waiters. Each cook had his own stove and cooked his own specialty. No one prepared more than two or three dishes, but there was still a great variety of Japanese food and tea and sake. It was all very cheap, and for a dollar or two a person could eat and drink until he was full. But the really unique part of the restaurant had nothing to do with the wonderful food or look of the place. In Rikko's restaurant any man, woman, or child had the right to get up and to "announce himself." A person would just get up whenever he or she felt like it and talk about him or herself. Everyone else would listen. Sometimes someone would answer, and maybe a discussion would take place.

I couldn't bring myself to announce. I'd be on the edge of doing it and I'd feel my heart go so fast, as if it would burst through my chest and run away by itself. I'd feel myself start to sweat, and I'd breathe so fast it made me feel like I would pass out. There were a few times when I had some sake that I thought I could do it—maybe not the whole thing—maybe just a short announcement: "My name is Ted. My father runs the drugstore. We live in back of the store. I can't stand grey days." But I couldn't even stand up. My legs got so weak, I knew they wouldn't hold me. Mr. Sotto told me that memorizing made me more nervous—so did setting a time or any kind of anticipating or rehearsing. He said that it split me. That one Ted would look and be the judge while the other Ted spoke, and that I was afraid of Ted the Judge. He said that if I did it when I felt like it, even if I merely got up and said "Hello"—or nothing at all—and sat down, I would do it as a "single Ted" and there would be no judge to be afraid of. But that feeling didn't come, and even though I tried not to wait for it, it still didn't come. Mr. Sotto said that trying not to wait was another kind of waiting, but doing nothing about it was very hard.

Other people announcing themselves didn't make me feel bad. Getting to know them and the food and light and the noise of the dishes helped me forget the greyness outside for a while. But there were other times when I felt so grey I knew just how Rikko felt when he told Mr. Sotto about killing himself. This, even though he had his restaurant and could stay in it and talk to people all of the time. Rikko would wander from table to table, sometimes talking to people, mostly listening. But it took him a long while to announce himself too.

THREE MONTHS AFTER RIKKO CAME to see Mr. Sotto, Georgy, Mr. Sotto and I had tea and cakes at the restaurant.

"I want to make an announcement," Rikko said.

"As you know this is the first time I've done this. I am Rikko and this is my restaurant. I have been troubled, deeply troubled. I have searched for weeks, in vain, for a garden within myself where I might find some rest, but all I found was deserts, empty deserts and terrible winds full of screams and moaning—awful moaning. Last night as I lay in my bed I got lost in terror. It was as if my struggles brought me to an awful truth. I had become a great emptiness. There was nothing left. Then it came to me that this place and you are my garden, and with that idea I was at last at peace."

For a few minutes he said nothing. There was absolute silence. Then Rikko spoke again. "I want to say that all persons who come into this place for as long as I live can eat and drink as they will. Pay what you will. And if you will, please pay nothing at all. You see I feel that a smallness in me which made me shrink into nothing at all has somehow melted. I no longer need to accumulate money. I am no longer Rikko, the small acquisitive person. Somehow I am free and I want to share this freedom with you. The smallness in which myself was hidden is now gone, and my being now occupies all of me. Perhaps I have become my garden. There are no longer separations in me. I am a whole person again as when I was an ignorant child. Please know that hunger is an alien enemy here. Share food with me and drink too. I Rikko, the man, am the same man I view when I look inward as when I look in the mirror. I am the man you see. There is only one man. The many roles I played are gone. I am no longer an actor with a frozen hidden self. My self is me and the empty actor is gone."

"But how did you do it?" a man's voice asked.

"I don't know," Rikko answered.

"How?" the voice persisted.

Mr. Sotto answered. "That you ask the question indicates that you are not ready for the answer. Eat the food Rikko offers."

"Will it help?" the man asked.

"It will help Rikko and it will help you," Mr. Sotto answered.

Late that night I asked Mr. Sotto if giving the food did it, and he said that it did not and that giving the food a night earlier would have been a meaningless affectation.

Georgy and I went fishing that night. It was actually at

four in the morning. The tide had just changed and we each caught a striped bass just before they left the surf to go out to sea. Together they weighed about twelve pounds. In the morning we gave one to Georgy's mother and brought the other to Rikko.

"I HAVE one small ability," Georgy's mother told us.

"You have many abilities," Mr. Sotto told her. "Perhaps you mean you have one unusual ability."

"I'm not sure it's unusual, but it's one which pleases me very much." How I loved to watch her talk, to listen to her voice.

"Tell us," Georgy urged softly.

"When I was a very small girl I made the discovery. If I looked very closely and concentrated very hard I could see flowers grow."

"You can see them move?" I asked.

"Yes—plants too."

"Any other things which move slowly?" Georgy asked.

"Yes. Watch and clock hands," she answered.

"How?" I asked. "How do you do it—is it just strong concentration?"

She thought about it for a while and then she said, "No, I was wrong when I told you that I concentrated. It's not concentration at all. It's quietness—deep quietness—the kind in which no disturbance exists at all."

"How does that do it?" I asked.

"I don't know," she answered.

"Perhaps it slows movement," Mr. Sotto suggested. "Maybe if we slow ourselves we can be in rhythm with the flower's growth."

"If we slow movement would we live longer?" Georgy asked.

"Perhaps fuller," Mr. Sotto said. "Open to feeling more of ourselves."

"Flowing slowly is the feeling," Georgy's mother said.

"Then if a person moves fast does he feel less?" Georgy asked.

"If he moves too fast he may come back to where he started from so quickly that in effect he doesn't move at all," answered Mr. Sotto.

"Perhaps growing and changing is quiet," Georgy's mother said.

"And growing is deep movement," Mr. Sotto said and after a pause added, "And is often so slow as not to be perceived."

I fell asleep that night without any thoughts or dreams at all. In the morning when I woke it was raining. Through the doors I could see the ocean clearly out to the horizon. The surf was very rough and there were thousands of whitecaps. Through the windows on the other side of my room I saw the bay. It was calm, and through the rain I could see that the tide was coming in.

AFTER MY FATHER CLOSED THE STORE for the night I made us some fried eggs and coffee. He wasn't tired and we talked. We talked about how he didn't like to go fishing though he did like to cook fish. He would stuff a bass with chopped up clams and small shrimp and then tie it back together with string and bake it. He also liked to make fish soup that was really more fish than soup—all kinds, whiting, bass, frost fish, weak, king, and clams and crabs too. On cold nights sometimes we'd have his friends Land and Accon over, and sometimes Rikko too, and eating the steaming fish and drinking a little bit of rye whiskey—Old Overholt was the brand my father valued most—warmed us nicely.

But on that night there were just the two of us in our big

all-around room—we slept and ate in it—back of the store, and the eggs, bread and butter, and coffee were as good as anything had to be. My father told me that maybe he was foolish, but that he was afraid that catching the fish would take away his pleasure in cooking them. He admitted that he enjoyed the cooking more than the eating—though that was all right too. I liked catching them—it was the second after they hit the hook just before I set it, when the line and rod vibrated the most, that was the best. Seeing them come out of the water was beautiful too, but it was also sad, because their color began to fade right away. I admitted that I could not club them over the head the way Georgy did, and letting them flop around until they died was not something I liked to think about. Georgy knew this, and so whenever we fished together he clubbed them all, though we never spoke about it. My father asked me how I felt about using live bait and I told him that it never bothered me, which was strange I suppose, putting a hook through a small live killy or sand eel— but that's how it was. We went on to talk about making prescriptions, and he tried to convey his pleasure in making them to me. Once I nearly had it when he poured different size empty capsules into my hand and then had me fill them by patting them down on piles of powders. We weighed out some powders on scales. He said that he liked mixing things in the different size mortars, and even more, pouring from different bottles into graduates, but labeling the final thing— all done into a bottle—was what he liked most. He used an upside-down bottle with gauze over the opening for his glue for labels. I can still feel the feel of the capsules in my hand today, and like I said, I nearly had the feel of his pleasure in it all then, but I'm sure not quite—no more than he could really get the feel of the fish when it jerked the bait in its nibbling vibrating way just after it took its first taste.

Somewhere along the line he asked me if Mr. Sotto liked

fishing, and I told him that he never went either. Then for no particular reason he thought he remembered that the Talmud says that one's first loyalty ought to be to a teacher even before a parent, but we never got around to talking about it. He asked if I wanted to take a walk and we went down to the beach, and when we got back I was tired and went to sleep.

"SOMETIMES THE RAGE I FEEL about death is so great, I feel that I'll break wide open with it."

"And then you go on," Mr. Sotto said.

"And then I go on," Rikko answered.

"But it all seems futile, doesn't it?" Mr. Sotto asked.

"Worse than futile—outrageous—a terrible trick played on me and by me in turn on my sons who will surely continue the farce by having children of their own. Yes, futile and outrageous. I could fall in love with life again, but then I'd be an even bigger fool."

"In life there is life—only life. One may just as well be the fool and fall in love with it."

"I once was, but no more."

"There are many kinds of love. Before I found the garden when I was forty-five my love was sharp-edged, very bright, quick, and broad. Now it is light, quiet, slow, and warm."

"Which is better?"

"Each is better in its way. The first is more intense, but always keeps in mind of the time when it will be over. The second is peaceful and a comfort and does not carry the forboding fear of termination with it. I suppose it is closer to death and to birth and therefore less in fear of its own loss."

Mrs. Sotto came into the room and she wore a thin, white, almost transparent blouse which clung to her breasts. Her nipples were little pinpoints through the cloth, but the dark circles around them were very large and I could see them clearly, and I felt Mr. Sotto's two kinds of love at the same time—the sharp kind and the quiet comfortable kind—and also a deep sense of loss and yearning. The yearning never quite went away—not even now.

GEORGY SOTTO LAUGHED the way all of us do, not at all like his mother and father. The sounds his father made were very low, but the laughing showed in his eyes. When Georgy or the rest of us laughed our eyes stayed the same or got smaller. Mr. Sotto's eyes got larger, and as he laughed he seemed to be seeing even more than usual and reaching out touching everything—yes, with his eyes touching us all even more than at other times. But when she laughed it was like a little child, because all of herself went into it. Her whole body laughed and her face glowed, but through it all the delicate feel of herself never disappeared. The graceful, elegant way she moved sped up as she shook with laughing, but she remained as gentle and soft looking as ever.

There were her hands. Mrs. Sotto shook your hand when you came into her house, and feeling her hand told you what she was all about. Her hand—and there was no separation between she and it as there is with all other people I know—was cool and warm at the same time. Her hand welcomed you and comforted you, just as her face did and her house did, and at the same time it told you that you were as free to go as you were to stay. Her hands were small and very finely made and soft even though she kept a garden. Her fingers were rather long and somehow looking at her hands could make you feel like crying, because anything so beautiful had to be fragile and vulnerable. But her hands also had a strength —or shall I say a gift or a power which was very special.

I arrived there in the late afternoon one day, a very grey day in which I could feel no sun or warmth, either inside me or outside. Walking on the beach to get to their house, I had the fantasy that I might be crushed by the heavy grey clouds before I arrived. But I got there and she shook my hand, looked at my face, and gave me a very tiny cup of sake. We then went to a small room in the very center of the house from which nothing outside could be seen. In that room, which I used to think of as the center of the world, the grey heaviness of the outside almost always disappeared. The room was very light and bright and painted in warm, smooth orange lacquer. There were a small black table and low black ebony chairs and small baskets of dried fruit and a little stove with a tea set. No one came there unless invited by Mrs. Sotto, so I suppose this was her room. I told her about greyness because this time the room did not take it away. It was there—holding me down and making me very sad. She then told me an extraordinary thing. She said that grey was a very beautiful color and that sadness was a beautiful mood too. She said that they both contained all the other colors and moods and that she saw greyness and sadness as the color and mood in which the other colors and moods rested and grew strong again, so as to burst forth for a while—like flowers in the sun—before going back to rest in greyness and sadness again. She said that when she was able to be very quiet in herself, the greyness and sadness became most beautiful because she could then see the other colors and moods. Yes, she felt that seen at home, or better yet felt, the colors were subtly and indescribably beautiful—much more so than when they burst forth, light and happy after their grey, sad rest. I understood her. I thought her words and voice and face told me all of it. But I didn't really understand until she held my hand, because then somehow the beauty of sadness went through me to my heart, and I was so full of it I thought I'd burst for joy. Going home that early evening the sky was heavier than ever and the grey light looked very forboding. But I imagined her hand holding my hand, and for a moment I thought I could see many colors and even bright warm sunlight resting in the thickening fog.

THAT YEAR the winter moved very slowly for me. It was as if nothing and nobody grew older during those months. It was a very harsh winter. At times the temperature dropped below zero and the Island was hit with gale force winds for weeks on end. Mr. Sotto spent a good deal of time mending the house, and Georgy and I helped him whenever we could.

One morning at low tide we found what must have once been an upper cabin of the superstructure of an old tanker. At first Mr. Sotto tried to build it on top of the house facing the ocean to make a kind of crow's nest of it. But the wind made it impossible and he said that he realized that it belonged attached to the veranda on the third level facing out on the bay. This room had a very special beauty, mainly because it was paneled in rich swirling walnut. It was only about seven by eight, but two or even three people could sit in it quite comfortably. Mrs. Sotto suggested that Mr. Sotto use it as a study, and he said he would, and we all immediately called it *Mr. Sotto's crow's nest study* from that time on. But it was never used for that purpose because Mr. Sotto did his thinking, listening, and talking wherever he happened to be at any time. Mrs. Sotto eventually put a straw mat in that room, and it became a place for anyone to stay and heal when things got especially hard and cruel—which sometimes inexplicably happens to people.

Rikko maintained his food policy at his restaurant but continued to struggle with inner turmoil. Though no one talked about it I knew that Rikko and sometimes his wife and sometimes both of them slept in Mr. Sotto's crow's nest study. I never slept there, but there was a morning when I spent several hours there looking out the window at the grey fog. For a moment of near dead silence I thought I could see beautiful colors in the greyness, and happiness in my sadness.

GEORGY'S MOTHER SAID that moods were symphonies of feelings, and that a discordant feeling changed the mood. When I asked her more about it she said that when our feelings were in harmony we were in a mood. If a particular feeling became too weak or too strong, the person became tumultuous because he was now in the process of forming and giving birth to a new mood, in which a new balance of feelings would be in harmony. She said that these changes were very rapid and were almost always happening, though most of them were so muted as not to be observed. She said that inner quietness of more than a few minutes duration was usually a rare thing, because prolonged moods or a balance of feelings were almost like the water in the ocean between tides; stillness didn't last long.

I asked where feelings came from, and Mr. Sotto said that they were there just as life was there—that they were the basic stuff of life. When I questioned further he said that a person is what he feels, and what he feels is him, and that there is no separation. He said that thinking with words about feelings is like thinking with words about music. Words keep us distant from the actuality. "To understand music we must listen and to understand feelings we must feel."

Georgy asked if a man is what he feels and if feelings and moods are always changing, then isn't a man always changing and really someone else every second.

Mr. Sotto replied that each man represents all the feelings and changing moods he has had in the now of his life. Each time he changes he is a different man, and the total of all the men he has been and all the changes he has gone through during a lifetime constitute the man he has been.

I asked what he meant by the *now* of his life and Mr. Sotto answered by asking how long was *now*. I said "even less than a second." Mr. Sotto said that it was usually much longer than that. "Now," he told us, "is as long as a man's life. His *now* begins at birth and ends at death." He explained that the division of time into seconds, days, months, and years was made only for convenience. I asked about the present and past, and how we could call what we have forgotten in the past *now*. He answered that we really forgot nothing and that we only made ourselves forget as a convenience, just as we divided the now of our lives into convenient time segments. He said that in certain moods we could be in touch with the entire *nows* of our lives—all that we ever experienced—all at the same time, and at those times we could feel life most clearly—but that this was very rare.

GEORGY'S MOTHER ASKED ME to ask my father to come along with her, Mr. Sotto, Georgy, and Mr. and Mrs. Rikko to gather small sea stones. My father closed the store and came with us.

To this day I don't understand why he closed the store and came. Up to that time he never closed. The store was always open day and night, and if someone came in and he wasn't available, they either took what they wanted and settled with him later, waited for him, or just came back another time. But this time he closed. I've thought about it many times since, and my only conclusion is that whenever he left the store and took a walk, as long as it was open he left a part of himself there and also took the store with him. I suppose it was always on his mind. But that day on the

beach gathering stones was different—and he must have
wanted it to be different because he closed the store and did
not take it with him and left no part of himself back there.
He was with us with all of himself the whole day. There
were times I was tempted to talk to him about that day, but
I never did and he didn't either. I think we both felt the
same way. That stone-gathering day was the way it was, and
any words analyzing how it came to be would have disturbed
the mood made by the memory.

Before we started out that morning we gathered in Georgy's
mother's kitchen—really a nice-sized but cozy eating and
cooking room all in one. It was quite cold outside and the
windows were steamed, and there was also cooking steam
inside. We had lots of smoked fish, all kinds, and hot tea as
well as a kind of brown steamed rice Georgy's mother made.
I watched my father because I knew he always liked rice so
much and I could see his surprise and happiness—he never
ate rice like that before.

Mrs. Rikko was very short and wide, and her face was
almost round as an apple. You could barely see her eyes inside
the two slits which closed completely when she laughed. I
used to think she looked like Eskimos I had seen in magazine
pictures. I mention her laughing because she laughed a great
deal, and even when she wasn't laughing she was obviously
nearly always in very good humor. But she was a serious
woman who helped her husband run the restaurant efficiently.
It was she who bought the best and freshest food and who
kept the many cooks organized. It was also she who every
few weeks introduced a new recipe, making eating at the
restaurant an interesting adventure. On this day she brought
a series of different sized baskets with all kinds of beautifully
arranged food in them: one contained compartments of different kinds of rice; another was full of delicately designed
pieces of dried fish; still another had pieces of raw fish, each

piece designed as petals of different flowers. And there was a small basket with glass flasks of sake and a little stove. These baskets fit together so that they were easy to carry and so that the different foods would not be disturbed until we were ready to eat them later on the beach.

Georgy's mother gave us each small cloth sacks in which to carry the stones, which were to be for her small garden. She had a large garden in back on the bay side of the house where she grew a considerable variety of vegetables during the warm months. The small garden was a resting place which consisted of a natural space between three wings of the house, a place Mr. Sotto said evolved naturally without conscious plan or thought when he put the house together. The small garden was outdoors and so it was not warm, but it was pleasant even in rather cold weather because it was almost completely protected from the wind which could only reach it from above.

Before we started out we asked Mrs. Sotto what kind of stones she preferred. She told us that any small stones were good but especially good would be those we gathered without thoughts—that is, without words in our minds. She said that the stones represented the impact of the sea on the land, and bringing them together in a small garden made both sea and land less fearful. Sitting in such a garden, a garden of ancient but newborn-looking stones gathered by friends, made one unafraid of vastness and infinity. This worked especially well if one could sit mindlessly and so become one with the stones and the universe. At this point she laughed and said that she was using too many words, and we went out to the beach.

We gathered small stones and said nothing. I thought nothing, and particular stones attracted me more than others. When words came into my head the stones looked alike. When I had no thoughts, different stones reached out in different ways to me. With some it was the color—pure white, translucent, a trace of red. With others it was shape, and with still others it was indefinable—they were just there and I knew they were ones to gather.

There must have been fish in the ocean because the gulls were noisy and concentrated on particular spots where they dived again and again. But fishing didn't tempt me. I knew the possibility was there but nothing distracted me from the stones. For the first time in my life that cold day on the beach I knew how deep and comfortable peace could be.

We ate at noon and the food was beautiful to look at, to hold, and to taste. We showed each other the stones we had gathered, and Georgy's mother said that she could see that we were mostly wonderfully thoughtless as we gathered them. We then went back to Georgy's house and helped his mother scatter little bunches of the stones here and there in her small garden. When she finished the garden was a more wonderful garden, even though there were no plants or flowers.

Later on we sat in the kitchen and had steaming bowls of fish soup and rice. I never saw my father's face look so peaceful and happy. We then had some dry fruit, sat silently for about an hour, and then also silently walked home.

"WHY IS MY WIFE CONTENT?" Rikko asked. "We share the same lives. There's nothing she has that I don't have. Indeed, she has me, a discontent, disturbed person while I have her, a content person. Surely, I should be the happier one."

"She is not at odds with mortality." Mr. Sotto answered.

"I'm not afraid of dying."

"You are enraged at your inability to transcend dying. Her humility saves her from the encounter with anticipation of death and the foregone conclusion of defeat."

"Do you mean she is humble and I am arrogant?"

"Since death is surely characteristic of all living creatures you do arrogate to yourself an attempt at power to supersede that which is characteristic of life and humanity."

"Then must I surrender to the insult? Yes, that's the word that comes to me—*insult*—but what I really mean is to death. Must I surrender to be at peace?"

"You have just stated your problem in the two words *insult* and *surrender*. Neither brings peace. Each and certainly both together must make for turmoil and despair. One may ask, shall you surrender to breathing? Are you insulted by breathing?"

"But breathing sustains life."

"Yes, but life includes death. In any case you choose a struggle which is unfair because it must lead to frustration and defeat. Because you know this you rage."

"Then I must stop struggling!"

"No! You must direct your struggle to your pride. You must struggle against the pride you would take in winning, and if you win in this struggle you will accept losing and you will win humility and the acceptance of life's limits so that you may enjoy living."

Rikko seemed pleased—hopeful—but Mr. Sotto looked perturbed. I thought perhaps he felt that he had said too much and had come too close to giving direct advice.

I saw Georgy in school but I did not go to his house as often for several weeks after the day of gathering stones. I think my father and I both had the feeling that we wanted to spend more time together. Neither of us said this in so many words, but when school was over each day I chose to help him in the store and he and I took walks all over the Island several times. There were also a few evenings we went to Rikko's for rice, shrimp, and tea. On one of these evenings I told him about Mr. Sotto's inner garden and of Rikko's inability to find it. He said that he thought he understood what Mr. Sotto meant but wasn't quite sure, because he thought this could also mean a kind of sick withdrawal from people and life. I said that I would ask Mr. Sotto.

"I THINK there is a difference," Mr. Sotto told me, "between a person who is forced into withdrawal and one who seeks quiet in himself through struggle with pride. I also think that each finds something quite different. One finds deadness. The other finds aliveness."

"In the garden?" I asked.

"Yes," Mr. Sotto answered, "in the garden. Aliveness is not a spinning maelstrom. It is found in the quiet peace of one's self. One must not mistake peace for deadness. There is great life force in peace—the very strongest kind."

"Ah peace"—Rikko sighed. "I think I have it and then I don't. I find myself in conflict again and again and still again."

"Of course you do," Mr. Sotto said. "Real peace is found in the ebb and flow of peace and conflict, and in the conflict itself. Your father speaks of 'sick withdrawal.' " Mr. Sotto went on. "If one is sick and must withdraw, then withdrawal is not sick but healthy. To withdraw may be a sign of feeling very badly, but the withdrawal itself is only an attempt to cope with the bad feelings and to gather strength so as to be able to emerge. But again, one withdrawal is for the purpose of terrifying oneself yet more than one is already terrified, with isolation and coldness and imaginary monsters and self-digestion. The other is to put the soul at peace against all attempts to destroy it."

"How can there be peace in conflict and struggle?" Rikko asked.

"By the acceptance of conflict and struggle and even by

embracing it with the understanding that it is a part of life too, and therefore must not be judged with pejorative equivocation."

I asked Mr. Sotto what he meant by "forced into withdrawal."

He said that forced withdrawal, unlike chosen withdrawal, brought one face to face with horror and fear—and rightly so, because even though there might be respite even in that place of hell from other hells going on "outside" one's self, it was nevertheless a monstrous place. Chosen gardens found through struggle against the terrors created by arrogance and pride were peaceful places with no self-created monsters in them.

I related this to my father as best I could and he said he thought he understood most of what Mr. Sotto meant.

IT WAS ONE OF THOSE UNEXPECTED DAYS in midwinter which sometimes happens by the ocean. Perhaps it is the influence of a stray current of warm ocean water which comes along and warms the land and everyone on it for a little while. Too, the sun was directly over us, round, full, and bright with no clouds or fog to obscure it.

We sat, Georgy, his mother, and I, in her small stone garden. For the moment the cozy feel of being inside the house surrounded by cold and fog was gone. The three of us were in a funny mood. I guess we felt light-hearted—bouncy and on the verge of giggling. We began to rearrange the stones. There were many more than we had placed there that stone-gathering day. Mrs. Sotto told me that she had continued to gather them every morning. Each of us went about arranging the stones in our own way. When we finished we sat down on small wicker chairs that Mrs. Sotto brought out of the house and looked at them. Even though we had worked separately without consulting each other, the entire garden looked as though it had been done by one person. She explained that this was because we were all in the same mood and that the stones reflected our mood. Georgy and I sat quietly for a while, and we both agreed that the stones did reflect our mood. Georgy's mother said that this is the way it usually is. Though we may think that outside things change our moods, it is usually the arrangement of how we feel that changes how we look at and even arrange outside things. This made sense when I remembered the many times I felt a particular way and then its opposite—like happy about the store and the back room we lived in and how wonderful they seemed to me. Yet there were other times where they hadn't changed at all, but they seemed poor and small and dark and depressing to me.

THE WARM WEATHER continued for several days. Georgy and I took the large rowboat out into the bay a few hours before dead low tide early in the morning. We stayed in the channel and took turns rowing to the flats in the middle of the bay. We were rowing against the current, and it took at least an hour and a half to get there. We waited for dead low and then hauled the boat up onto the mud among the reeds, now all out of the water and a dark winter brown. The reeds grew over our heads and was extremely thick in all directions, but there was a path among them that was about twelve feet wide and ran for several miles from one side of the flats to the other. There were also large outpockets entirely free of reeds in several places at right angles to the path. The reeds never grew over these outpockets, and however low the tide got there were always little rivulets and shallow pools left behind in them between tides. These outpockets were always full of periwinkles, killies, tiny hermit crabs, occasional blueclaws, and small mussel clusters. The largest consisted of a big clearing among the reeds and was situated about a mile and a half from where we left the boat. This was the place that had the best soft shell clam beds in the bay. It remained that way because no one ever took baby clams or too many of the large ones at any one time. Some kingfishers and terns scooted about the edges of the flats, but no gulls were flying. Though it was still unusually warm, there were clouds and some mist too.

We were quite sweated up by the time we got to the clam beds. The first thing we did was to dig for sea worms, but we found none at all. Sea worms were like that—they could be there by the dozens or just suddenly disappear and there wouldn't be any, not even one. We then went poking around, just looking over all the busy creatures swimming, digging, and scurrying around the tide pools and small streams. Doing this, we found a few blue-clawed crabs that were big enough to put in our clam sacks. We played around like this for a long time. The influence of the warm weather lulled us, and we forgot all about time and tide. We went on this way for several hours and then explored the reeds adjacent to the clearing to see if we could find other clear areas. We finally found another area relatively clear of reeds some distance away from the clam bed, which was particularly marshy and in which the ground was almost pitch black. A number of eels slid about in the shallow pools and black mud, and we spoke of coming back in the spring to get eels for Georgy's mother to smoke. A good deal of time had passed since we rowed to the flats and we finally went back to the clam beds and filled our sacks in a very short time. As we did, a memory occurred to me of a time a few years earlier when Georgy and I got our boat stuck on the flats during low tide. We had come out at mid-tide, rowed directly into the middle of the flats, and suddenly found ourselves high and dry at dead low

—also having lost track of time. At that time we fortunately had Georgy's small boat so we did not have to wait for the tide to change. We went ahead and pulled and pushed the boat back to the channel. Small as the boat was, we worked very hard and still it took us several hours.

The memory of this incident while we were clamming startled me out of the dreamy mood we had drifted into. I realized that much time had passed and that the tide was rising very fast. I told Georgy and we set out for the boat immediately, understanding that we had also been fooled by having been on relatively high ground, for the path was now rapidly filling with water. I had a fantasy of the boat drifting off, but I said nothing to Georgy. Before we got to the entrance of the path we were wading in mud and finally swimming. We were still a considerable distance from the boat when Georgy suggested we let go of the sacks of clams so that we could make better time. We did so at once, and even in the middle of what had now become a fearful predicament I wondered whether the clams would make a new bed or find their way back to their old place. I also wondered if we would ever see our own beds again. And then there it was—the boat had drifted into the reeds close to the opening of the path and fortunately had held fast there. By the time we got to it we were exhausted, and the boat was beginning to free itself as it floated over the tops of the reeds which now just barely showed.

It took us quite a while to row back to the Island because we were still somehow going countercurrent, and because we were exhausted from the struggle to get back.

That night I slept without dreaming, but before I fell asleep it occurred to me that pleasure could turn to pain and life to death with hardly any notice at all.

.   .   .

SEVERAL WEEKS LATER Georgy and I told Mr. Sotto about the incident.

He said that we would always remember it because it was our first deep encounter with the haphazard quality of nature and existence.

I remember shivering when I thought of the huge expanse of water and the tides and how ruthless it all was and how small and fragile we really were. Then I thought of Mrs. Sotto telling us about the stones making us less afraid of the ocean's vastness. I went into her small garden and sat alone among the stones for a while and felt better.

ONE COOL MORNING in the early spring, Georgy and I met a man on the beach painting a landscape of the beach and ocean. Georgy was interested in the painting itself, but I became mesmerized by the paints. The artist, a very short Japanese man we never saw before or since, had a beautiful wooden box divided into small compartments, each containing small lead tubes of oil paints. Each tube was labeled according to the color of the paint it contained. I vowed to myself that I would soon have a similar box of tubes of different color paints. We watched him paint for a while, and then we left. But the idea of the need to own the paints persisted.

I found a set of paints, not quite like the artist's, a few weeks later in a small store near school and my father gave me the money to buy it. I spent several minutes every now and then looking at that set of paints over the months, but I never opened any of the tubes; painting couldn't have been further from my mind. I never even associated the paints with painting or pictures or works of art. I was intrigued with the tubes and happy to look at them, touch and feel them, sort them out, and arrange and rearrange them periodically. At one point my father suggested that perhaps I ought to paint something before the paints dried out. I still remember the pang of pain the idea of the paints drying out produced in me. But this in no way mobilized me to paint. Indeed painting was something utterly alien, unthinkable and, even more important, unfeelable.

When I spoke to Mr. Sotto about this matter he said that there was no reason to paint, or to think about reasons to paint or to not paint, or to speculate about the significance of what the paints meant to me. He said my feelings about the tubes of paint were enough and all that mattered.

I did not lose touch with those special feelings related to the paints, even after the paints and tubes dried up and even years later, after the box was lost.

"MY SLEEP IS BETTER," Rikko said.

"You are letting go," Mr. Sotto replied.

"I am not in charge so much anymore."

"Is it a relief?" Georgy's mother asked.

"A great relief," Rikko answered.

"And the nightmares?" Mr. Sotto asked.

"Less ominous," Rikko answered.

After a while Rikko asked how sleep could improve still more and how dreams could become less fearful. Mr. Sotto said that embracing dreams—even the frightening ones—and loving them as part of ourselves made surrender to sleep less fearful. He also said that "surrendering mastery" and "trusting ourselves to nature's benevolence" made sleep welcome and pleasant. Rikko asked if this would help with death too, and Georgy's mother said that "perhaps death can be seen as a return to nature's protective arms and warm bosom." Rikko said that it was hard for him to envision death as "warm and protective." Mr. Sotto replied that this was hard to see until one moved from the position of "mastery of self and life" to "surrender of self to life." At that time, he said, "nature would reveal its kindness" and death would be felt as "nature taking you back into itself and into harmony with all that is."

Rikko smiled and said that for the moment he was content that his sleep had improved.

"IF ALL OF ONE'S SELF is used at the same time, there is less opportunity for the self to separate into parts and to contemplate each other. Self contemplating self is the stuff of pride and harsh judgment, and any activity which seems as though it would make for this splitting becomes rightly terrifying."

I asked Mr. Sotto if there were activities or exercises which reversed this process.

He said there were certain activities but not exercises. He felt that exercises were contrivances which did not use the "whole self at the same time."

I asked what he meant by "whole self at the same time" and he said "being one with what one is doing—continuous and inseparable from the activity itself." He went on to say that this is what artists do—they are one with the art activity. He gave dancing and painting as examples, and also carpentry and just driving nails into wood. He said, "To the artist carpenter, the hammer and the nail and the wood form a whole being—they are all one." He said that the dancer in dancing is the dance and the picture the artist paints is the painter. He said that when I held and sorted my tubes of paint and felt the way I did, those feelings brought split selves together. He told me that laughing was very good too, but that by laughing he meant non-forced and non-contrived or partial laughing, "Whole, full, spontaneous laughing which draws the whole self into it leaving no part out." He said that he saw Mrs. Rikko do this a few times, but only a few times. He said Mrs. Sotto did this now and then. I pictured her laughing and how her whole body laughed but how she at the same time lost none of her graceful self—in fact became even more of it—and could feel the meaning of what he told me.

I danced. I knew nothing about dancing but I danced. For several weeks I got up very early and went to the beach and danced. At first it seemed odd because I didn't know what to do. And then I let go. Something in me came free and I felt light and easy and it seemed to me that I could jump around, leap, run, and swing about in the most wonderful way. One morning I understood Mr. Sotto. All of me was in it. I moved a different way. Ted the judge was gone. I could move freer and easier than I ever imagined, and one night I announced myself at Rikko's.

I just got up and said, "I'm Ted. Georgy Sotto is my friend. Rikko's food is good," and I sat down and I felt very good.

I stayed over at Georgy's house that night and when I woke early the next morning the winter and greyness was gone. It was spring.

The bay was like a mirror—absolutely still—and the water was green. The ocean was calm too and looked very blue, almost violet. The sunlight came from the bay and the ocean into the house, and my room was flooded with bright light and warmth.

WE WALKED ON THE BEACH that day, just Georgy's mother and me. I still remember the sand crabs burying themselves with their hind legs as they burrowed down into the sand, and the little tracks they left. There were also bubbles here and there left by clams digging down deeper into the hard mud. Kingfishers ran up and down the beach on their thin super-fast legs, just beating each new wave as it came in. The seagulls seemed happy just to glide about in long swoops on the currents of warm air; they weren't diving for fish at all. The beach looked very clean and the ocean was calm and bluer than I've ever seen it before or since. And the sand was white and Georgy's mother was pale and beautiful and walked so delicately—so very delicately as she moved her hands and talked. I said that I once had seen mountains a long time ago with my father and that they were very beautiful, but that I had never seen the desert except for pictures in books. She said she once saw a desert when she was a very little girl, and mountains, too, and that they were all beautiful. But the ocean, she said, was special. It was a living entity full of living creatures and all of it—the ocean and everything it contained, from the minute one-celled animals to the giant whale—was alive and always in motion. I told her that our blood was isotonic with the water of the ocean and tried to explain what this meant—molecular concentration and so forth. She understood and I said that the ocean was the blood supply for many of the smallest beings, supplying food through their cellular walls, as our blood does for the cells of our bodies. I told her that we came from the ocean and that blood was our internalized ocean which freed us from the ocean and permitted us to live on land.

We must have walked for miles. She spoke of whales and her special affection for them. As a girl she had the fantasy that all the oceans of the world had secret connections and that whales knew where they were and went from one ocean to the other. She also fantasized that they lived more in a world of sound than of water and that they could discern changes in sound and could communicate with each other over vast distances. I told her that I had read something about whales and that some of what she fantasized might be true. She wondered about the size of these giants and we both recalled how several had been washed up on the beach several winters earlier. She thought perhaps their huge size made for more acute hearing—all that skin surface acting like huge ear drums, able to pick up sound vibrations. And then she laughed and said that all of it was pure fantasy and that I should not confuse her love of whales with knowledge of them of which she had none. I didn't care at all. I only knew that I loved her.

THE SPRING WENT MUCH FASTER than the winter, and the summer was soon with us and it was quite hot. But it never became too uncomfortable because there were always breezes off the ocean and the bay. Some mornings I looked out across the beach and tried to imagine what the desert would feel like, but the sound of the ocean intruded.

Now that school was over I spent a good deal of my time helping my father in the store and clamming on the flats with Georgy. One day we walked to Land's End Point where a narrow stone jetty marked the southernmost end of the Island and the bay met the ocean. We walked to the end of the jetty and fished the incoming tide. We caught stripers, sea porgys, and fairly good-sized black fish, more than seventy-five pounds of fish. It took us about five hours to lug them back to Georgy's house. When we arrived Mrs. Rikko was there, and she and Georgy's mother said that they would make a huge fish soup and would serve it with rice and sake at Rikko's restaurant. Everyone all of us knew was invited. This dinner took place two nights later.

I never ate anything so good and I never ate so much. We'd stop for a while and then we'd eat some more. My father, who usually ate very small portions, ate almost as much as I did. Once again he had locked the store and was completely with himself and his eating at Rikko's that night. And then he surprised me because he got up and spoke.

"My name is Nathan. You know my son Ted and my friends Rikko and Mrs. Rikko and the Sottos. I run the drugstore. This fish soup is wonderful."

MY FATHER WAS DIFFERENT after that evening. He was less tied into the store. He took more frequent walks, locking the store after him. He talked more and seemed easier about things. Customers noticed that he spent more time talking to them and seemed happy to hear whatever they had to say about themselves. He also asked his friend Sam Land over more often, and they played chess and spoke of old times and drank hot tea. My father and Georgy Sotto's father drank hot tea no matter how warm the weather got.

It was a cool, quiet summer and helping in the store, fishing, and eating in Rikko's now and then made the days just slip away so that we were into the fall and early winter hardly knowing how we got there. I felt happy looking forward to spending cold days and nights in Georgy's house.

AND THEN ONE DAY all of it was gone. I caught a cold that early winter which turned into pneumonia so that I had to go into a hospital on the mainland. When I got out my father told me that the Sottos were gone. All the Japanese people were gone. Many went to relatives in California. The war had begun some weeks earlier and the government, when it got around to it, took all the Japanese people away. We, too, left the island shortly after that and I never went back.

PART II

When I Decided To Feel Everything

WE first met him in a crowded elevator in Geneva. He took out a blank cartridge gun and shot everyone in the face. The Swiss were not amused, but we both laughed and so the three of us had coffee in his favorite café. I paid the check.

In the middle of much laughter and getting-acquainted small talk, he told us some very personal things. I interpreted this as an effort to quicken the pace of our becoming friends of some importance. He told us of a memory which troubled him all of his life.

He was four years old. He was playing a game with his father. They were laughing and having a wonderful time. It was raining outside. His mother was cooking in the kitchen. It was cozy and he was very happy. Without warning his father hit him. He hit him again and again. He lost and regained consciousness and his father was still beating him. He was in bed with multiple severe injuries for several months. His parents hovered over him. For a time there was some question as to whether he would recover fully. His parents were now dead. He said he never bore either of them any malice at all. The incident bothered him only because he could not understand what touched it off. He remembered no arrogance on his part, no disagreement, no bad words between them at all. His father never touched him again. He was as caring and as affectionate as before the beating for the rest of his life.

He went on to tell us that he had been divorced a few years earlier. He had two children who lived in another canton with their mother and he seldom saw them. When they divorced neither of them wanted the children. There was a custody battle. He won and she got the children.

That night, on the train back to Lausanne, I told her of two incidents in my own life.

I was twelve years old. There was a retired army officer who lived close by. He was famous for liking children. We spent many hours talking about war and soldiering. I thought I was his favorite. One evening I was part of a group of perhaps six of us listening and talking to him. He suddenly pointed to me and I still remember the words, "You have a beak for a nose—do all Jews have beaks?"

We had to stay over in the city to visit a sick relative. We stayed with an aunt. She unfolded a tiny bed in the kitchen. They insisted that my sister sleep in a regular bed while I slept in the small folding bed, though I was much too big for it. They said it would have to be that way because even though my sister was much smaller, she was older than I, and I was a boy. I sat up in the kitchen all night and in the morning made sure they knew I didn't use the bed. They showed no sign of pain.

She told me about being sick as a very young child and having to be carried upstairs because the doctor prohibited use of the stairs. One day she was carried in the presence of children her own age. She said out loud, "I wish I was dead." It was the only time in her life she was slapped by her mother.

Then we talked about him again and realized that his telling us about himself had worked. We had saved a good deal of time. We had our first friend in Switzerland—an instant but real friend.

THAT DAY I WOKE UP and knew that I was a collector of cunts. I wanted to see them, all kinds, close up. The word itself excited me, and the idea of seeing them brought on feelings that were almost too much to bear.

In the peep show on Forty-second Street there were little

curtained booths, at the bottom of which I could see the lower half of trousered legs like in the pissoirs in Paris. I went into one and drew the curtain fast, afraid to be seen.

I faced a small glass window covered by a metal shade. A sign told me to put a quarter in the slot and to pull the lever. There she was, spread-eagled under four powerful spots, slowly revolving on a platform. As I waited for the turntable to bring her crotch into view, I noticed the staring eyes through the other windows around the platform.

My excitement and curiosity vanished. I looked at her face and breasts. Could she see us? Could the other people see me? Who was peeping at whom? She couldn't see anything! She was busy wiping sweat from her face and shielding her eyes from the lights. Then I saw her cunt. It was sweating too. There was a trickle dripping from it, forming a small puddle between her thighs.

The curtain dropped. I was in the pissoir booth again. As I left, a man walked out of another booth. We quickly turned from each other. A beautiful, elegantly dressed woman quickly walked out of still another booth. She pushed us both aside and disappeared into the crowd on the street. A man with a small camera took pictures of the place and the people as they left. I too ran and got lost in the crowd.

On Broadway and Forty-seventh Street I climbed a narrow staircase, paid five dollars, and went through a turnstile into the middle of a show. A naked girl strutted around the stage mechanically shaking her small breasts every few seconds and following with a few pelvic grinds and bumps. After a few minutes she stopped and straddled an elderly bald-headed man, keeping one foot on the stage and the other on the arm of his seat. Then she peed a few drops on his head. All of our eyes were on him. His face was brick red. He looked up smiling, and the urine dripped down his neck into his collar. Everyone started to laugh. He reached into his pocket, I thought for a handkerchief, but he pulled out a bill—I think ten dollars—and gave it to her. Then she headed in my direction. All eyes were on me. I got up and ran out.

Another place much the same down the street. A girl, nude, on the circular stage, nondescript and vacant eyes. Then she was on the other side, back to me, legs spread. Two men, flashily but expensively dressed, carefully looking up her crotch and then grinning broadly, approvingly, clapped their hands in unison. Everyone but I took up the cue and clapped. A man in the seat next to mine poked my shoulder and whispered, "clap" and I clapped in rhythm, too. Then she was at the edge of our end of the stage, bent backwards on all fours, legs apart, and we—the men on my side of the stage —clapped harder and faster. Her cunt closed and opened, closed and opened in rhythm with our clapping. We clapped faster and she opened and closed faster. Then she could no longer keep it up and fell back flat on her back. Her legs crossed. An elderly man appeared on stage and gently helped her up, covered her with a robe, and guided her behind the curtain. I heard someone whisper, "You know, that's her father."

Still another place. A small-faced, big-eyed, thin, flat-chested girl pleaded with us, appealing to those of us who were too shy to sit up front to "please move up closer so you can see it all." By twisting her legs in pretzel-like gyrations her vaginal slit took on all kinds of funny facial expressions. We all clapped and with heartfelt appreciation she said, "Thank you, thank you," over and over again. This made me very sad and I left. My cunt collecting day was over.

I'D HAVE DONE ANYTHING for a hamburger. I passed an outdoor place called Toto a dozen times. The owner, a short Japanese man who lived in the same rooming house as we, saw me, but he didn't invite me over. Somehow people peppering their hamburgers made me particularly crazy. I thought I could smell the meat and pepper and I couldn't get it out of my mind. I walked up and down the boardwalk and then back to Toto again. The man just stood there, king of his hamburger stand, and said nothing. For a second his broad grinning face looked like a hamburger. But I didn't want to bite it. I had the fantasy of sticking a knife and fork into it and cutting it up. The craziness of the thought frightened me and I ran up the boardwalk again.

I came to a hoop-the-prize place. Watches, clocks, vases, radios, and other items were set up on little pedestals, and the idea was to hoop a prize and get the hoop clean around the pedestal. The name on the sign above the place was G. Costas. G. Costas tried to sell people a chance on winning a hooped prize as they passed. Now and then someone stopped and bought six hoops for a dime, but they never cleanly ringed a pedestal. G. Costas periodically fitted a hoop around a pedestal to show it could be done but nobody was able to do it from the required distance.

Then G. Costas saw me watching and motioned me over. He asked if I would work for him for a couple of hours and I said yes. My job was to stand there and throw hoops. Every once in a while I circled a pedestal and "won a prize." I couldn't understand how I succeeded while all the others failed. There were quite a few who tried, attracted by my winnings. When he finally closed the place that night, I returned the prizes and he gave me a fifty-cent piece. Then he showed me the hoops. Mine were about a fifth larger than the others.

I ran back to Toto. The place was closed. I went back to the rooming house with the fifty-cent piece in my pocket.

. . .

I JOINED THE CROWD. It was large and continued to grow as other curious people joined it. The man refused to get out of the taxi. The driver pleaded with him, but he refused and got abusive. Between curses and screams of "Jew-bastard" he punched the driver in the head. The crowd got larger, but none of us interfered. I was in the middle but could see over everyone else's heads. I was paralyzed. "Get a policeman," the driver pleaded, but we didn't budge. Now the man had an arm around his neck and punched him in the nose with his other fist, yelling "Dirty fucking Jew" with each punch. Blood streamed down the driver's forehead into his eyes.

Suddenly, someone pushed me aside as he shoved through the crowd. He was short and husky. He was out front in a few seconds. He jumped into the back of the cab. He punched the passenger in the face several times. I thought he would stop, but grasping the man's hair, he held his head up and methodically, rhythmically, beat his face into a pulp. Then he got out of the back of the cab and pushed the driver to the side and started the motor. "Where are you going?" somebody yelled. "I'm bringing the son-of-a-bitch to a police station," he wheezed. I wondered inanely whether he was asthmatic or just out of breath. As he drove slowly through the crowd we all spat on the man through the window. I heard someone say, "That will teach you to say 'Dirty Jew'!"

Going home on the train I thought of the short man and the battered face of the anti-Semite and I felt exhilarated. Then I thought of the blood in the taxi driver's eyes and I felt ashamed, guilty, and embarrassed. I recalled the drugstore my father owned when I was a small boy. One summer evening a huge drunk man stood in the small square surrounded by ours and other stores. He harangued the Jewish storekeepers and shouted obscenities and curses on the Jewish people. He insulted us in every possible way. But everyone, customers and storekeepers alike, remained frozen at their windows. My father's face was white and I felt confused and terrified. A policeman finally arrived and subdued the drunk with a single blow to the belly. I couldn't understand why my father hadn't protected us. I had seen him throw insulting customers out of the store on many occasions.

Just as the train pulled into my station I recalled a still earlier incident. I must have been three or four years old. My father received a letter from Europe and sat in the bedroom crying for hours. Years later my mother told me that letter carried the news that my father's father, a man renowned for his gentleness and wisdom, had been pulled off a train and beaten to death during a pogrom.

"IT'S AN ORDINARY PENIS."

"I don't believe it."

"Believe it!"

"I can't."

"It's neither large nor small."

"But different!"

"Not in the least."

"You don't like me."

"Nothing to do with it."

"It must be different."

"Why?"

"Because you're different."

"That's a myth, too."

"No! I know it's true. You are different. I just want to taste it."

"You can't."

"But why not?"

"It's out of the question."

"Are you uptight. Is it guilt?"

"Perhaps."

"After all your years of analysis you still worry about guilt?"

"I suppose so."

"Are you really so hemmed in—so conventional? I won't bite it off."

"The thought never occurred to me."

"Let's say I have an obsession. Don't you want to cure my obsession? After all, I am your patient."

"No."

"Just a touch then."

"No."

"A look."

"No."

"You're afraid I'll be disappointed!"

"Maybe."

"I know I won't be. I can't believe it."

"What?"

"That just a thin piece of cloth separates me from it."

"Do you believe that?"

"Of course not. Do you think your wife would mind?"

"I don't know."

"But you would."

"Yes."

"Do you think you'd like it?"

"I'm sure it would feel nice."

"Then why not?"

"You tell me."

"Must be the cloth and all the pretense that goes into making the world the idiot place it is."

HE ALWAYS SEEMED DEPRESSED. Never said a word. Waited for my order, no sign of recognition, downcast, gave me what

I asked for, took the money—no hello, no goodbye. But he made good sandwiches and the place was pleasant and clean, so I ate there several times every week.

One day he asked if he could sit at my table. For several minutes he said nothing at all. I thought he was going to have one of his own sandwiches, but he just stared at the wall behind me. Then he started to talk—with obvious hesitance, difficulty, and embarrassment, eyes still on the wall.

Our Conversation

"Someone told me you're a doctor."

"Yes."

"A psychiatrist."

"Yes."

"Were you ever in the service, Doc?"

"Yes, the navy."

"I was in the navy, too. Sometimes it was rough."

"Yes."

"Lonely."

"Many times."

"Thing happened once."

"Oh."

"Can't get it out of my mind."

"In the navy?"

"Yes, all these years. Sometimes can't sleep."

"What?"

"Never told no one."

Then he blurted it out fast.

"A guy sucked me off. I let him. We were alone for a month. Just us stationed alone. The Aleutians. He asked me. I let him."

"Not unusual."

"Not unusual?"

"That's right."

"Does it make me queer?"

"Homosexuals are people too, you know."

"I know but I don't want to be one. All these years because of that, just that, I've been thinking I'm maybe one."

"It doesn't make you queer."

"You sure?"

"I'm sure."

"Then why? Why did I do it?"

"You were lonely."

"It's true. I was lonely. They would have kicked me out of the navy if they knew. Jesus, all those years."

"All that self torture."

"I feel better." He smiled and looked so much younger. "Jesus, I feel good."

"Fine."

"Thanks, Doc."

"For what?"

"You're the only one I ever told."

Each time I returned he was all smiles, greeted me, and said, "See you tomorrow, Doc," when I left, but he always looked at the wall behind me.

HE HAD TO SELL THE HOUSE. We loved it, but he had no choice. We had to leave the furniture, too. Selling it "furnished," he hoped to get a better price. Besides needing the money, we knew we wouldn't be back for a long time.

Our house was in a direct line with his property, and he said he was buying ours so that he could have more land, and to put up guests.

Price and terms were agreed upon immediately, but then he wanted a complete inventory of the furnishings. My father told him that we were leaving everything except books and clothes, and he seemed pleased. Then he mentioned the two fishing rods and reels. There was nothing unusual about them, but I had had them since I was a child and my father told him we were taking them along. He wouldn't hear of it. He was adamant.

He wanted the fishing rods or the deal was off. "A deal is a deal," he said. He reminded my father that he had already said that everything but books and clothes was included. He said that he didn't care about personal effects like jewelry or personal photos, "but that fishing tackle was part of the deal." We had no jewelry and my father told him that I had had the rods for years and automatically thought of them as "personal effects" and counted on taking them with us. But he wouldn't hear of it. My father tried to tell him that he would buy him new rods, better ones, but the buyer said the discussion was over and that he couldn't spend any more time on it. Walking out he said to let him know—"either the deal is a deal or the deal is no deal, but everything's got to go with it."

We had no choice. Time was short, we needed the money, and we couldn't take the risk of waiting. He was paying a fair price, and we convinced ourselves that the whole thing was silly. I could buy other rods for myself. The man was obviously crazy and we would have to go along. My father made the deal. But I was sorry immediately after he signed the papers. I felt a sense of loss. I just couldn't believe it was the rods. Maybe it was leaving the house and everything we owned. But it was the rods, and the sense of loss when I think of them is still strong.

I've bought so much fishing tackle since, but it's never been the same.

· · ·

I SAW THEM FROM A DISTANCE and wondered what it was all about. When I got closer I realized they were standing in front of a synagogue.

Everyone seemed highly animated and enthusiastic. Soon I was among them. They were mostly young people and were all wearing their very best. It must have been an important holiday. One girl in her early twenties was a great beauty by any standards. Tall, large high breasts, small waist, thick long black hair, large blue eyes, beautiful nose, mouth, chin, long legs, exquisite hands, dressed elegantly, moving ever so gracefully. She was radiant. I couldn't stop staring, and other people in the crowd milled about her and glanced and stared too.

They seemed to talk at the same time, hands and fingers and eyebrows and eyes and mouths moving, and all were looking at the girl. When I was right in among them I realized they were making no sounds except for an occasional high whine or grunt. They were mutes—deaf mutes. I was in the middle of a crowd of deaf and mute people. I opened the door of the synagogue. It was crowded with people. The rabbi conducted the service in sign language and the cantor, too, "sang" in hand signs. The congregation responded with hand motions.

I turned back to find the girl. She was all smiles for a serious thin young man who spoke to her with rapid excited hand motions. His hands and fingers were delicate, long, and graceful. Their movements were quick but were also fine and sensual. Off to a side sat an older man, about fifty, short, thick set, with unusually broad shoulders. He watched them intently. Neither of them saw him. The girl answered the young man. On her left hand she wore a unique silver and gold twisted wedding band. It looked familiar. I looked at the older man's hand. He wore the same ring. They were husband and wife.

It may have been something the young man said, or perhaps it was his persistent attention to the girl, that caused the husband's anger. His jaw muscles worked rapidly and his face was very red. The girl looked nervous. She turned this way and that but she still smiled and didn't walk away. At one point she looked directly into my eyes and the effect made me dizzy.

Then the husband was with them. He must have been extremely fast. I hadn't seen him move. All eyes were on them now. Nobody else was making speech movements. I still don't understand how all those deaf people knew so quickly that something was "going on." But they did, and everyone listened intently with their eyes. Meanwhile people were walking by across the street and a voice and a few words drifted across now and then, oblivious to the silence in front of the synagogue.

The man hit her a resounding whack across the right side of her face. She turned very pale and his red welted finger marks stood out clearly in the sun, still shining brightly on that clear day. The picture of a branded horse came to mind but quickly dissolved with the girl's tears. Her face was wet with them and her eyes swam in them and her shoulders heaved up and down with soundless sobbing. She was more beautiful than ever. My heart raced so that I could hear it in my throat. I felt bad. The man punched the young man in the face very hard. I thought I heard his nose crack but it was his glasses. They were shattered. I had the flash thought, "deaf, dumb, and blind." The young man, using his fine fingers, delicately picked splinters of glass from his face. There were tiny bleeding points around his upper front cheeks and the husband punched him again hitting the beautiful hands, glass, and cheeks. The young man's face was full of blood and tears but I could see that he wasn't maimed in any way. Now the girl was shouting. Her mouth was open and her neck muscles strained but only high pitched tiny sounds came out.

The husband spoke with his hands to the young man, then to the girl who continued to scream her soundless screams. The young man turned and, pushing through the crowd, disappeared. The husband took his screaming wife's hand and pulled her away. As he passed me I could see tears streaming down his face. There was absolute silence.

The street across from the synagogue was empty.

HE WANTED TO JOIN OUR CLUB. He should have stayed out.

He was the only one we knew who managed to get a job in the country for the summer. He was going to be a general helper in a camp for sickly children.

We decreed that he would have to be initiated if he wanted to join. This was only because he was the last one to join and we were bored.

We couldn't decide on the initiation.

I finally thought of a haircut.

We all pitched in. When we got through, his head was a mass of patchy tufts.

When he reported for work they were afraid he suffered from a contagious skin disease and sent him home. We called them and spoke to them and wanted to send him to a doctor to prove to them that it was our haircut and not a rash at all. But this seemed to convince them all the more of his "skin disease."

He spent the summer in the city with the rest of us, and I'm sure his deterioration started then and there.

"WOULD YOU LIKE to put your tongue in my mouth?"

"No."

"Wouldn't like it or don't want to do it?"

"Neither."

"Kiss my nipples?"

"No."

"Liar! I'd like to put my tongue in your mouth. Would you like that?"

"No."

"Masculine crap."

"No."

"False teeth?"

"No."

"Do you have false teeth?"

"They're capped and I do have a partial bridge."

"There! I've scratched your vanity after all. But then I knew it all along."

"What?"

"Capped teeth, partial bridge—but your vanity—you mark the difference, don't you, between partial bridge and false teeth?"

"I suppose so."

"You're as vain as I am."

"Maybe."

"I'd still like to put my tongue in your mouth. Is this love talk?"

"I think it is."

"Do I arouse you?"

"No."

"But in a small way—a very tiny way—I have succeeded, haven't I?"

"I'm not sure."

"Well, I'd like your tongue in my mouth. So far no success there."

"Is that what keeps you coming here?"

"Maybe."

. . .

WE SAT AROUND THE TABLE in back of the store that last night. I'll never forget the bottles on the shelves, the smell of the medicines, the small scale for weighing powders, the mortars and pestles, the dark shelves and wood paneling, the old wire-back chairs, the sink, the overhead fan stilled because it was winter and very cold outside, and my father's white face.

He told us he was closing the store. "Walking out!" Business had come to almost a complete stop. People had no money so they took their prescriptions to the new cut-rate chain stores. There was no more room for small drugstores. No one wanted to buy his. He would just walk out. The four of us sat at that table in the back room and cried. It's the only time I remember us all crying together.

Then he told us he was going into the secondhand business. He knew of a good location in the city. Since he needed five hundred dollars and had only half, he was going into partnership with another druggist. In hard times people bought secondhand things, he reassured himself. My sister and mother asked him secondhand what. Secondhand everything, he answered—clothes, furniture, umbrellas, fountain pens, everything, anything. They started to cry all over again and so did my father, but not I. I felt disloyal but it sounded like fun, all those things. After he closed the store that night we went back to the rooming house and no one said a word. Weeks later I realized my father's drugstore was gone forever. I never went back to the place where it once stood.

IT WAS VERY HARD to get him. It took all kinds of connections, and I called everybody I knew. He was one of the most talked about performers of that time. Getting him was very important. It was a guarantee of a great attendance, which meant money for our cause, and we needed money. When I finally spoke to him he agreed immediately. He had never spoken to a banquet group but for this cause he said he could not refuse. He was in complete sympathy. He understood our needs. He wanted to help in every way possible. I assured him that his presence alone and just a few simple words would be of immeasurable value.

His name brought more subscriptions than we ever dared hope for. For the first time we had money enough to go on. As hard as times were nobody turned us down. We rented larger ballrooms three times before the great night itself arrived, and we were finally oversubscribed for the largest room in the city. But people refused to be turned away. They consented to stand, to go without dinner, just to glimpse him, to hear him speak.

When he got up the applause was deafening. They waited for him to speak. He looked as he did in pictures, in newspapers, and films. The crowd seemed to purr in satisfaction just to be in the same room with him. But he stood there and said nothing. We waited one minute, two, three, and still he said nothing. People shifted about. Their silence was broken by a whisper here and there, giggles from different spots in the great room. Then he opened his mouth and absolute silence was restored at once. "This cause," he said, "this cause." He repeated the two words several times and said nothing else. I was on the dais so I could see the sweat dripping from his face. I gave him some water. The whispering started again. I made out giggling too. In giving me back the half-glass of water, his hand shook so badly he spilled most of it on me. The giggles turned to loud laughter. He smiled and ran off the platform and out of the place. Someone yelled, "Bum." Others took up the cry. Some woman started to clap. Others clapped. There was a mixture of clapping and shouts of "Bum!" and "Phony!" that went on for ten minutes.

Others spoke. The audience applauded. No one alluded to him. Everybody seemed to have forgotten him or that they came because of him. We all ate whatever food was put before us and then went home. On the way out I heard one woman say, "Maybe it wasn't him, maybe it was an imposter." The newspaper told of his "disgrace" the next day, but gave no reason for it. We had a lot of money now and sent him a letter of thanks. His own career went rapidly downhill, and in a short while his name disappeared from public view altogether.

A HUGE GREEN TRAILER TRUCK never left the street. Every night, after ten, I saw men of all ages dressed in every conceivable way go into the truck and then leave it a few minutes to a half hour later.

After several weeks my curiosity pushed me past my shyness. I asked a man passing by what it was about. He told me that they went there for "sexual relief." Men lined one side of the truck. Other men crouched on their knees before them. Anyone was free to choose whether he wanted to be a "standee" or a "crouchee." My informant told me that he shifted positions every few evenings. He also said that the truck was pitch-black so that no one saw or could recognize anyone else. It was all done by "touch and feel." The unspoken rule was that as each man entered he must make certain that no one else was entering or leaving so that there would be no chance of recognition. I asked him who the truck belonged to and if the police knew. He said the truck was provided by a very rich woman who was known to befriend homosexual men. This "fag hag" also knew the neighborhood authorities and made sure that it would be safe for all concerned. He never met the woman but was sure that she was "a great lady."

I asked him why they cared about recognition inasmuch as the recognizer would also obviously be homosexual too.

With poorly hidden contempt he told me that this wasn't the point at all. He explained that people didn't want to be recognized because needing the truck meant that one was incapable of meeting someone on his own. I asked how he could feel that the woman who provided what in effect was a "put down" was "a great lady." He told me that he felt this way because relief to those who could get it no other way was more important than pride, and that if recognition was avoided one could have his pride, too. With considerable iciness, he told me that he himself never needed to use the truck, forgetting that he had just told me he shifted positions in the truck every few evenings.

I FELT ENRAGED and despondent. Both feelings combined to make me sullen. When I left the city years earlier I had promised myself to never go back. All my associations relative to the place were gloomy and forbidding. My memories as a child there were full of rain, greyness, cold, and confusion.

Reports had it that the place had deteriorated even more. Old people had been stabbed, strangled, and beaten to death for a few pennies. Women had been tortured and raped. Children had been burned and thrown from roof tops. A population of mixed racial groups had turned on itself, and no act seemed grotesque enough to satisfy its self-hatred. But I had no choice. Business forced me to go back this one time.

I decided to rent a car and to take along an old fishing knife. Then I felt embarrassed about being unduly frightened and paranoid. But I finally took the knife and kept it on the seat beside me.

The night I arrived it was as it always had been. The streets were dark, dirty, and grey, and the heavy rain was the same as that of my childhood.

Halfway across the city I stopped for a traffic light. An

arm shot through the window and formed a strangle-hold around my neck. "Money," the arm's voice said, "money." I could hardly breathe but managed to reach the knife. The hold on my neck tightened and then I saw the man's nose. It looked enormous. I put the knife on the bridge of the nose and started to cut through in a back and forth movement. He choked me harder. I felt my chest burning and my head pounding but I kept on sawing. I could feel the knife going through the gritty cartilage. Neither of us stopped. We were caught in a kind of hideous pride deadlock. Then I felt the knife cut through. In a flash of lightening I saw the face. I had cut his nose off. He screamed and let go and I drove off, the knife beside me again.

Later that night in the hotel I recalled an incident that I thought was gone forever. It was during the depression. We lived in a badly run-down rooming house. My parents and my sister had not returned, even though it was dark out. I was alone in our room. I heard screaming in the hall. I ran out. Six Japanese men lived in the room across from ours. One of them ran toward me with a towel in his hand and blood streaming down the side of his face. He opened the towel and there was his ear. He asked me where there was a hospital. He wanted his ear sewn back on.

After I returned the car, I realized that I had forgotten the knife. I decided I would not go back for it.

"DON'T YOU WANT TO TASTE ME?"

"No."

"Have you thought about it?"

"No."

"Will you give it some thought—some feeling?"

"No."

"Is it because you are married?"

"I don't know."

"But you once admitted to me that you had been a collector of cunts."

"Did I?"

"You know you did."

"So I did. But that was for less than a day and a long time ago."

"Strange you should have told me about it."

"You asked if I had feelings like that."

"Mine is particularly nice."

"How do you know?"

"I saw it. I feel it, I just know."

"I'm happy for you."

"Why?"

"That you feel so nice about yourself."

"Is that where you think myself is—in my cunt?"

"Why not? It's as good a place as any other."

"So you don't want to taste myself in concentrated form?"

"Could say that."

THE BAG was the important thing. We focused all of our attention on the bag. My father acted as if it would in some way give me protective status. Secondhand suitcases were hard to find. A lot of people were going off into the army and navy. Perhaps they felt the same way too. We finally found one that suited us. It was a yellow-orange cowhide. Because it was genuine leather it was very heavy even though it wasn't that big. The smell of it was good. It had a squat kind of bulldog shape. Maybe it wasn't status at all—maybe he thought it would establish home wherever I'd be. It had that solid, implacable look.

Just before I got into the lineup and on the train, he patted my shoulder and then he patted the bag and walked away. That night, I dreamed he told the bag to watch out for me.

When they gave us sea bags a week later I had to send it home. I was relieved. It had been so heavy.

THAT WINTER I worked for a home maintenance service. Getting the job was a great victory—everyone I knew wanted it. I was very proud of my white coveralls. Since I was the youngest one in the crew I wasn't given that much to do. Many of the houses were closed up for the winter.

My job that week was dusting.

They left me off in front of the big white mansion and I let myself in. I went from room to room dusting and looking at hundreds of rare objects. It was like a lavish museum.

Then I thought I heard sounds. I went into the room. There they were, a naked man and woman vigorously making love on the carpet. I recognized her. She was the owner of the house. They glanced up and saw me and went right back to their work. I noticed a cat with a big red ribbon wandering about too. I dusted a few pieces and then left the room.

I felt degraded but I didn't know why.

HIS GREATEST JOY was baiting the Vaudoise police. The fact that they were the epitome of Swiss efficiency challenged him.

Until it bored him he considered his "film campaign" one of his most successful "embêtement exercises." He would casually wander into photography shops and steal films waiting for processing. Later on he either deposited the films in other shops or exposed them and sneaked them back to their original source. For a while the Swiss kept his campaign a secret: it could hurt the tourist business. They warned storekeepers to keep unprocessed film off the counters, but old Swiss habits are not changed easily and his success continued. After several months stories of the "film thief" appeared in newspapers. He proudly showed me clippings. Tourists complained bitterly. Films of arduous mountain climbing feats, honeymoon remembrances, second honeymoons—motion and still pictures—were destroyed or impossible to find. Columnists suggested that an anti-Vaud ring was at work, perhaps involving agents from another canton. He continued "operations" on occasional trips to other Swiss cities. Geneva, Berne, Montreux, Sion, Basel were all his victims. The Vaudoise police were getting nowhere. People became suspicious of resorts across the Swiss borders. Could the Italians, Austrians, or the French be involved? Then it all stopped abruptly. He told me that he had won and there was no point in going on with it. He was bored.

His trips to our house from Geneva, where he lived, were never ordinary. He made great efforts to create suspicion from the moment he left the train station. He slinked along the streets, suddenly changing pace, walking, running, standing still, staring. He charged into apartment houses, quickly taking elevators to the top floor and then walking down the staircase and sneaking out the front door again. By the time he'd arrive at our place he'd often have several Vaudoise policemen following him. They'd wait in the street, sometimes for hours, until he left. He would carry on the same way back to the station. He felt very happy when on several occasions they stopped him and questioned him. His papers were in order and they could find nothing wrong. They never questioned his strange antics. Professional police pride did not permit questions related to why they considered him suspicious. Of course they never connected him to the "crise aux films," as it became known before he let up.

One day he came to our place needing a shave, starved, and

quite depressed. He had "won." He was sure of that but they had been unfair, "pas correct" as the Swiss would say. He felt they had cheated and he knew that he could no longer play the game. They had picked him up two days earlier as soon as he arrived at the station. They told him they were taking him in for questioning. He could not have been happier. At the police station they locked him into a small, absolutely bare, windowless room and told him to wait. He "waited" without food, water, or a toilet for forty-eight hours. He told me that it was the most horrible and wonderful experience of his life. After several hours he had intermittent terrifying hallucinations and nightmares. He felt buried alive, and at one point was sure he was dying of a heart attack. But through it all he knew how badly he had beaten them and this sustained him. When they finally returned, they looked at the puddle of urine in the corner with great contempt. They let him go and told him that they would "question" him again any time his behavior was suspicious enough to warrant it. They conceded nothing at all of defeat. After he ate, shaved, showered, and napped he went back to Geneva.

WE WERE STATIONED IN THAT CITY for three months. The townspeople hated sailors and we were lonely. We were free every night but there was nowhere to go. There was a vaudeville show in town that had new acts every week, but the dozen semi-dressed girls in the chorus line worked there permanently. They remained on stage in various poses throughout the show. During specialty acts they posed in the background; between acts they danced very awkward dull routines, and were completely out of step with the music and each other. Policemen were stationed on both sides of the stage to protect the girls, if necessary. This seemed highly unlikely. It was a terribly boring show but six of us went there three times a week. There was nothing else to do. The place was always full and the audience always applauded appreciatively.

We devised a game.

We arrived early enough to sit in the center front row seats. We paid no attention to any of the acts or to eleven of the girls; we concentrated our complete attention on one pretty girl just left of center. We never took our eyes off her. She never indicated in any way that this affected her in the least. We then stared only at her left breast. This went on for some three weeks and still brought no response. We doubled our visits and went to the show six nights a week. She still did not respond.

Between shows we had discussions and even arguments. Two of us felt defeated and wanted to surrender. One of the defeatists even wanted to send her flowers and a note conceding defeat. We reminded him of the townpeople and their hatred for us and our recent information that the girls were townspeople, too. This rallied us for a while. One man thought we ought to change girls, but I pointed out that this would constitute a defeat. Another of us couldn't tolerate the idea of weeks of wasted work on the girl. One man proposed sending anonymous letters and another suggested we wear some peculiar item even though this would be against navy regulations. Still another thought we all ought to grin at her foolishly but in exactly the same rehearsed way. This last suggestion was taken with the most seriousness, but we finally decided these were all forms of cheating and smacked of defeat. We finally arrived at a kind of compromise conclusion. Nobody really believed it would work and one man thought it was cheating, too, but we dedicated ourselves to it. We would all stare as one at the dead center of her crotch.

We went and stared night after night and the strain was enormous. The sessions left us both tense and exhausted. Two men could only relax afterward by drinking very heavily. But our investment by this time was overwhelming. We were determined to see it through if necessary until we left the town. She did not respond. We discussed other tactics but again decided to go on. There was one night we thought we arrived too late to get seats, and this created considerable agitation. From then on we went dutifully to work each night, even though her expressions remained utterly flat.

Then it happened, three weeks before we left town.

We were staring as usual at her covered vagina. No response. We were half asleep, paralyzed with boredom, feeling like catatonics. The chorus was doing one of their simplest routines. For a moment they stood still, arms flung out in a greeting to the audience, accompanied by a few seconds of silence from the orchestra—an attempted high spot we'd been through dozens of times. She pointed at us and screamed in rage, "Fucking sailors! Fucking sailors! Fucking sailors!" The show stopped. She stood there pointing her finger at us and continued to scream the two words again and again. At first the audience did nothing and neither did the people on stage. Then the people from the stage and orchestra started beating us. People in the audience, taking the cue, joined in. Fortunately the whole situation was confused so we weren't as badly hurt as dazed. Through it all we continued to hear her scream, "Fucking sailors." The two policemen must have called reinforcements because in a few minutes there were a score of them. We were thrown out of the place and told to never return. We were bruised but jubilant. We had won and we didn't have to go back.

THE TWO CITIES were four hundred miles apart. The land between was empty and grey. Since there would be nothing to see I decided against taking the day bus. The night train had no sleeping facilities but I was tired enough to sleep sitting up.

The two men woke me twice, brushing my shoulder as they went to the toilet. Halfway through the journey I woke again to terrible screaming. Several of us rushed to the toilet. The door was locked. The screams were now moans. Someone said two men were locked inside. We pounded on the door. A deep voice said, "I'm not through yet." The moaning stopped. After a few minutes he opened the door. It was one of the two men who woke me earlier, splattered with blood. The other man lay under the sink in a pool of blood. We dragged him out. His face was a red pulp. His nose and cheekbones were crushed. His eyes were closed shut by swollen flesh. His lips were split in several places. "Fucking fag tried to blow me," the splattered man said.

They stopped the train. Two men carried the battered man to a small house near the tracks. After the train had traveled another fifty miles we realized the splattered man was no longer on the train.

I fell asleep again. I dreamed of the first time I assisted in a leg amputation. It was above the knee. He told me about the importance of getting a good flap and stump. When he sawed the sound and smell of burning bone made me sick. When I got back from the bathroom, the leg was off. I had to carry it to the pathology lab.

IT WAS a three-hundred page ordnance manual. It was full of computations explaining complex gunnery systems, and it demonstrated breakdowns and reassemblage of the fifty-millimeter machine gun, the forty-millimeter antiaircraft gun, the twenty-millimeter surface gun, the three-inch fifty, and the five-inch thirty-eight. It explained in detail electronic feed in information and connections to activating mechanical systems. To me it was a massive jumble of integrators, cam plates, muzzle velocities, trajectory curves, and all kinds of electronic circuitry which in no way ever came together, so many disconnected symbols. I was incapable of understanding any of it. It had to be learned by each officer candidate. Failure meant dismissal from the program.

I memorized it in detail, every nonsense symbol. I had no choice; I wanted the promotion. Life in the navy was much easier as an officer. I memorized the manual day and night. I never went out on liberty. I hardly slept. I was involved in the most boring and arduous exercise of my life. But I felt heroic doing it, and I did it in full.

I received a hundred percent in every examination. Other candidates asked me to explain ordnance problems. I couldn't. They hated me, convinced that I refused them out of malice and competitive motives. My instructor called upon me several times to demonstrate problems and their solutions at the blackboard. I couldn't. He said in view of my brilliant performance on the examinations I was obviously a very modest person who was just too shy to show all I knew. For a moment I almost believed him myself. My classmates hated me even more—this despite my telling my roommates that I was actually an idiot savant. I spent a miserable last month in the school. The class received the news of me being one of the only ones exempt from the final examination with stony faces. I had paranoid dreams involving assassination. By the time we left the place I was almost completely ostracized.

WE PLAYED BANKER and broker and gin rummy. I kept winning. I won consistently. I couldn't lose. For a while I felt that I was endowed with special ability. As I accumulated money I insisted on playing for higher stakes, and after a while no one could afford to play with me. I stopped playing. I felt my time was too valuable to waste it on small games. I finally gave up banker and broker altogether and switched to rummy. I did even better at gin. I convinced myself that gin rummy was a game of skill. Periodically, someone new would arrive. I'd beat him too. Then they all chipped in to back new players. After a while I started to play full-time again.

All of them hated and respected me. I loved it—their hatred and their respect. I bought food with the money and shared it with them. This elevated me to new heights of hate and respect. I was separate from the rest. The winning made me an outsider. I became known as *the winner*, just that—*the winner*. Someone offered to be my slave. I paid him. He made my bunk, polished my shoes, arranged my games. At times I forgot I was in the navy.

Then I became bored. I couldn't stand the game. Sitting and playing for hours became torture. My eyes burned. My back ached. Memorizing the cards played made me nauseous and gave me headaches. I couldn't stand it. But when I quit for even a day I'd begin to feel that I was just one of them. I couldn't stand it, the lack of distinction. They'd start to like me, to treat me like one of themselves. Two, three days away from gin and I craved their hatred and respect. I needed it desperately and I'd go back to it, and nausea. I finally left the place and was saved.

"You're like he was."

"How so?"

"Implacable."

"But you stayed so long."

"I needed him. Like I need you perhaps."

"For what?"

"The implacability. The stone wall effect. Immovability. An existential force."

"What did it do for you?"

"A sense of self. It gave me a sense of myself. Of human limitations. It didn't diminish me. Made me feel more human. Then I couldn't stand it anymore. Never being able to budge him. Like you. I'd like to budge you."

"Then you would lose interest."

"I wouldn't. God—how I'd love to be in love again. To feel excited. That feeling of anticipation. Waiting for him to come home. The one who makes your heart dance. That waiting is the sweetest feeling there is."

"Yearning. At least you feel that."

"Yearning. Yes, I guess that is better than nothing. Because after him I felt nothing at all for so long."

FOR A WHILE my job was to open and sort out old, sealed trunks, barrels, and suitcases they bought in auctions. His partner was the inside man and my father, who said that the years of being cooped up in the drugstore had left him restless, was the outside man. He went to apartments and bought anything people who were moving wanted to sell. He also bought from people who were going out of business, and occasionally from people who came in off the street.

Some of the auction houses sucked up the city's secondhand things and then distributed them to people like my father. The sealed trunks, barrels, and suitcases came from transport companies and storage houses. He never bid more than the price the empty trunk would bring: the contents were the profits. Their stock included anything anyone ever owned. It was all there: desks, clothes, books, pens, tools, furniture, clocks, watches, paintings, umbrellas, plants, scissors, bicycles, statues, knives, uniforms, handcuffs, guns, clubs, luggage, pots, pans, light bulbs, soap, brushes, false teeth, eyeglasses, machinery, cameras, film, binoculars, silverware. Sometimes they bought single objects. Other times they bought things in the thousands. At one point they had eight thousand broken dishes, five thousand ballpoint pens, fifteen hundred umbrellas, and two hundred right-footed galoshes. Sometimes, in buying out a dying business my father would bring in a load of new goods. For a while we had a vast assortment of condoms, handkerchiefs, and the ball point pens too. They were new. Once, I opened one very large trunk full of canned food and jars of pickles and jams, and for a time we both ate and sold the food. One small trunk was full of marijuana. My father recognized it and gave it to the police, though his partner was sure they could sell it for a great deal of money. Several trunks were full of old, rotting garbage and one had a large, dead, grey rat in it. One made a terrible stink and turned out to be full of manure. One had sixty new one-dollar bills falling out of the lining. After that I made exploratory slits in all trunks with linings. I had to be careful because we still had to sell the trunks. Sometimes I found diaries, old pictures and neatly tied packets of love letters. Some of the letters still carried the scent of perfume.

The store was situated near the very busy theatrical area of the city. All kinds of people came in. There were customers for everything—it was just a question of waiting long enough. On several rainy days we sold the umbrellas and galoshes. The pens were regularly forty cents and we sold them two for a nickel, so they went fast. A stage show in town needed dishes to break every night and bought all our damaged dishes, and so it went. We learned to throw nothing out. Eventually everything got sold. One day a man came in with an eleven-year-old boy and paid a dollar for an old pair of knickers and galoshes which fit the boy perfectly. They couldn't contain their joy. My father was there at the time and he threw in a pair of socks, woolen gloves, and a scarf. They were speechless. The man hugged and kissed my father. The boy got into his new old clothes then and there. My father's partner dug up two old, torn sweaters, one for each of them. They put them on and the man kissed him too.

One evening I found a pornographic book in one of the trunks. I left before they closed and read it on the way home in the train. I got very excited. When I reached my station I couldn't get up. I knew the bulge in my pants would show. I went station after station far past my stop. I put the book down and read it, put it down and read it some more. We came to the end of the line and the train started back again. I was on the train for hours. When I finally finished the book the bulge wouldn't go down. Then at one point when the train was very crowded, it started to vibrate. The vibrations reached my groin and I had a violent orgasm. I could feel my face go brick red and very hot. I was sure other passengers knew. But I was finally able to leave when I got to my station. When I got home, very cold and sticky, they had all been asleep for hours. The hot shower felt good. In the morning no one asked me why I got home so late.

EVERYONE PRETENDED to be very important—it was that kind of party. I was as pretentious as the rest. At first I resisted and was myself, but everyone's embroidery and exaggeration was too much. We both turned fancy too. Even our speech changed and we talked in a very profound manner about things of which we knew little or nothing.

The hostess was very proud of her cooking. Inappropriate to the rest of the pretense, the food was meat and cabbage, simple and good. Cabbage never agreed with me, but by this time I must have been convinced that my stomach changed with the rest of my evening's metamorphosis, so I ate it. At the table there was more talk, pretentious gesturing, and much manneristic behavior. The food remained the only honest item. No one said anything about it, but along with the acting we ate voluminously and I ate great quantities of cabbage.

Driving home we were still full of false dignity and cabbage. On the expressway I began to get cramps. At first they came and went every few minutes. Then they were upon me every few seconds. Soon they were continuous and violent. I asked her to drive the car. I could hardly get out and walk to the passenger's side. The cramps enveloped me completely. Deep excruciating waves of gut pain radiated down my thighs almost to my ankles. My belly felt like it would split down the middle. My total effort was concentrated on keeping my rectum from letting go. There was no gas station in sight. I thought of stopping on the side of the road but I think I was still trapped in my evening's pretense. I told her to go "faster, faster," and then "slower, slower." The pain was terrible— like pointed knives and hammers in my belly and legs. Then we were on cobblestones. I couldn't stand it. But there it was, a gas station in the distance, and I told her, "faster, faster, make a run for it," and she did, and we went over a series of still larger cobblestones and something in me jolted and I let go. "Too late," I told her and in seconds I was inundated in explosive shit. I was swamped with it, dripping in it, and the relief was enormous. I laughed with joy. We both laughed hysterically so that she could hardly drive. I sat in it covered from head to toe all the way home and we were so happy to be ourselves again.

IN COLLEGE, he was our genius. There was no question he couldn't answer. He amiably explained all problems in math, physics, and chemistry, and read to us history, economics, political science papers, and English themes offering valuable suggestions. No professor ever stumped him. We called him "the think machine," "essence," "encyclopedia" and just plain "genius." The amazing thing to us was that we never saw him study. We used to say he was really a hundred years old and did all his work in his first fifty years. He told us that he did it all while he was still in elementary school. In high school and college there was nothing left for him except to help the rest of us.

He was particularly attentive to premedical students. Though he cared nothing at all to be a doctor, he respected their ambition and sympathized with the great difficulty involved. He stayed extra hours helping to perfect their lab procedures. Finding *unknowns* in qualitative chemistry was the most difficult term project in the school: only a handful of people were able to succeed on their own, and the genius got the others through. He took minutes to do lab reports that took everyone else hours, and always lent us his results to check our own.

Nobody was ever jealous or envious of him. It wasn't just his altruism, but it would have seemed grossly inappropriate to envy someone who seemed to us to have come from another planet. His ability was so superior and foreign to the rest of us that envy would have seemed insane. I think it never occurred to us, though among the rest of us competition and envy were common. Competition with him would have been futile. Even if another genius would have popped up among us there still would be no competition because "the think machine" had no ambition whatsoever. He was bored with school and had no desire to go on with any professional training. He enjoyed taking us through and that was about it.

Many years later I saw him. I was on my way to my office and I passed a big chain drugstore. There he was in the middle of a small crowd of customers demonstrating all kinds of tricks with a yoyo. He told me that he was very unhappy until the yoyo. It was the only thing that ever challenged him. Mastering it involved hours of work each day and took more than a year. He finally won several important contests. This got him the job of yoyo demonstrator for the chain of drugstores. He was happy.

.

SHE WAS A FORMER PATIENT, a beautiful lady. At first I visited her at home several times a week. Then I went to see her in the hospital. She complained of severe pain in the upper right quadrant of her abdomen. Sometimes it radiated to her right shoulder and became excruciating. She said it was "like air hitting the exposed nerve of a tooth."

Seeing her in the hospital room felt strange: she belonged in the lavishly furnished apartment that had been her home. When she first arrived at the hospital her beauty and elegant manner were still intact and enough to convert the hospital room to a home—her home. But as disease destroyed her, the power of her beauty diminished, and with each of my visits the hospital room became increasingly just that. I re-called how when she was my patient, her presence used to change my office. The power of her being there had been enough to convert it. Each time she entered my room, my room became her home and I was the visitor.

Now the hospital room had become a hospital room. Neither of us was at home. That she should die away from home in a blank room seemed intolerable. I visited her hus-band at their apartment to talk to him about this. Without her the apartment was no different than the hospital room. The beautiful furniture, oriental rugs, and paintings could have been part of any fine department store furniture section. I never brought it up to her husband. We spoke briefly of her condition and I left.

On the way home I thought about our "secret agreement." Without words we had established an ironbound contract.

Neither of us would ever mention the fact of her malignancy. In subsequent visits, morphine no longer contained her pain. Before she died she moaned continuously. The hospital room was a bare dying place.

"ARE YOU DEPRESSED?"

"Yes."

"I could tell. Is it bad?"

"Not good."

"Want to talk about it?"

"No."

"Doctors get depressed, too, then."

"Surprise you?"

"No."

"Scare you?"

"No. Can I help?"

"Being here helps."

"Would you rather I kept quiet?"

"No."

"Would you like me to hold you, rock you, cuddle you?"

"No."

"Excite you? Lots of men think I'm very exciting."

"I don't doubt it."

"Do you feel taken advantage of?"

"No."

"Because here I am trying to take advantage of you while you're down."

"I know."

"Does it make you angry?"

"No."

"Do you think it will last long?"

"I don't know and I don't think of how long it will last."

"Masculine strength crap?"

"Maybe, but I don't think so."
"Just depressed and will last as long as it lasts."
"That's about it."
"Do you think I'm beautiful?"
"Yes."
"Thank you."

WE LOST A LOT OF MONEY that night. At first we won. She played roulette and I played chemin de fer, and we rushed over to each other between plays to tell of each victory topping the preceding one. We had fists full of small round chips and her purse and my pockets bulged with large square ones. Sitting there at the table saying "Banco," "Avec la Table," "Suivi," elegance and affluence suffused me.

At one point we took a break and shared cold langouste dipped in heavy french mayonnaise, cold chicken, and chilled Swiss white wine. Even the casino host came to our table to greet us and to learn our names. Later on we found out that his great talent and job were to permanently memorize the names of all the casino patrons and to greet them personally forevermore. My cards came up eight, and nine several times, too. During the height of the winning I walked to the roulette table. She had chips on the seventeen and carré. I put additional chips on the seventeen, carré, chevaux, on the black, manque, impair; and seventeen came in making all of our bets winners.

Other people realized we were large winners. A small crowd gathered to watch each of us play. We felt very special and we continued to win. People bet the way we did and they won, too.

Then we started to lose. The crowd drifted away. Soon we lost it all. The boat across the lake had stopped running hours earlier, so we pooled what money we had left with two other couples and hired a limousine to take us all around the lake and back to our place. Traces of exhilaration lingered; mixed with the relaxation of losing, our mood was one of decadent elegance. In the darkened limousine, the other people relived their gambling plays of the evening. I put my hand under her dress and between her legs. At first she resisted. Then she closed her thighs tightly around my hand and in the middle of much gambling talk I could feel her orgasm. By the time we arrived home, the sun was shining brightly. We had croissants and coffee on the terrace and then went to sleep. It had been a beautiful evening and neither of us mentioned it again.

ON THAT DAY I woke up and knew what purpose she served.

I met her in my first week at college. I was in the grip of an instant powerful at-a-distance crush. Our relationship never developed. We met and talked now and then and there is where it remained. During one conversation I realized that she had a cruel streak, and this shocked me. I didn't want to know anything more about her. It might spoil the sweet excitement and purity of my obsession. Instead, I'd see her at a distance, wave hello or goodbye, and think and dream about her constantly.

I met a girl. We made love. We shared everything. We grew older together, and I kept the "college girl" locked in time and place in a corner of my mind. She never grew older, never left the campus, never married, never had children. She was my *then*.

What if? What if we, too, went to bed, shared problems, grew older? How would it have been? These questions provided a kind of romantic aura which could not have existed had we really shared human substance together and had I been able to answer them.

That was her purpose for me. She was *then* and *what if*—poor stuff compared to the richness of all that happened since then, and almost nothing at all relative to now. But, there she sits waiting for the rare moment or two to be called upon to provide *then* or *what if*.

"YOU'RE BETTER NOW."

"Yes."

"Wasn't a real depression after all?"

"Real?"

"The kind we real people get."

"What a snob!"

"The kind that hangs on day after day after day. You get up in the morning, your eyes aren't open yet, you think there's a chance it's gone. Your hopes rise. You open your eyes and there it is sitting on your chest, weighing you down, laughing at you."

"Yes."

"Yes, no, your two favorite words. At least you're not a grunter. I have a friend who goes to a grunter. But I'm glad you're over your depression."

"Thanks."

"You mentioned yearning. Do you know how it is to yearn?"

"Yes."

"I mean deep inside to have a yearning that eats your insides up and you can't satisfy it. Do you know?"

"I do."

"Come off it. You can't know. You've got it made. Big shot doctor. It's what you wanted to be, isn't it? You've got your wife haven't you? You've got your children. . . . What do you know about yearning?"

"Quite a lot."

"You probably always had it made. You secure people get

to me, you really do. You're all the same, smug. Smug! I suppose I'd be smug, too. My feelings would all be in place, too, if I had your background."

"My background?"

"Oh, I know, I know nothing about it. I mean the hard facts of it. But I know in my guts that it must have been a very safe secure one. I mean what can you, a doctor, know about it? You people are all the same. Your lives are so nice and orderly. And you tell me you know about hunger. You know about taking shit? You know about how fucking violent and crazy life can be?"

"Yes, I do."

"From books. Tell me, you think you have no pretenses."

"No."

"Thank God you admit that. Listen, before I leave I want to apologize. I know I've been a bitch but I just feel that way, that's all. Please don't even answer me. Whatever you say I'll feel patronized. Don't even say so long or I'll see you next time or anything like that. I think I'm disappointed that you're not still depressed.

How did we demean him?

We gave him a haircut. We continued to do other things too: once begun we couldn't stop. He had become the person to whom we did things. We never thought to stop.

We put him on a bicycle and he couldn't ride. We were going to teach him. But he took off and rode away. We found him a half-hour later. He told us that it went well but he didn't know how to stop or turn around. He finally crashed into a wall.

We went to a roller skating rink. He couldn't skate, but he did skate. He did so by clinging and bumping into everyone else on the crowded rink. He manged to stay upright for quite some time while he knocked almost everyone else in the rink down—even the best skaters.

This and other events made first-rate comedy—not unlike some good slapstick movies. But there was nothing intrinsically funny about him. Had he been a comedian this stuff would have been nourishing and aggrandizing. But he was a serious fellow, and we didn't treat him seriously. The effect was demeaning.

THEY TOLD ME that the operation went well. I believed them. I felt comfortable. I even joked with the man in the next bed. His surgery went badly. An artery had been cut in his scrotum, and it was the size of a large grapefruit. It had also bled into his penis which looked like a huge, blown up frankfurter. They were blood red and rested on a gauze bridge constructed between his thighs. There was nothing to do for him but wait for the blood to be reabsorbed, which would take several months. He told me that he was known as the man with the red-hot balls.

On the second morning I started to cough. I also noticed my belly getting hard. I felt bloated. Each cough brought terrible pain which began in the incision and radiated through my abdomen and strangely into my armpits. The man with the red-hot balls told me to call the doctor, but I refused. I thought it would go away—but it was more than that. The hospital and staff intimidated me. I foolishly had made up my mind to be a "good patient." I didn't want to bother anybody. But the coughing continued and the pain in the incision now stabbed down like a hot knife into my back. The pain in my armpits had no time to subside between coughs. It was there all the time. I was on morphine those first days but it didn't help.

One day it reached a point in which I coughed without

letup. The man with the red-hot balls pressed the buzzer and eventually the nurse arrived. He whispered to her and she gave me codeine pills. For a while I thought these helped control the cough, but then it started all over again.

He pleaded with me to call the nurse and the doctor. I told him to mind his own business, but I was in agony. Then when I coughed, I felt something in my belly give. I felt better—the pain wasn't bad at all. I reached down and felt under the light outer gauze dressing for the inner dressing. It was no longer there. I pressed down with my fingers and found it. It was deep down into the incision which was now wide open.

The pain was completely gone but in that moment I felt indescribable terror. I opened my mouth to scream and no voice came out. Then I managed to blurt out some disconnected words. My hands were behind my head. I didn't dare put them in the vicinity of the incision. The man with the red-hot balls pressed the buzzer, but no one came. I coughed again and then several times in an uncontrollable burst. There they were, my intestines, reddish blue and terribly bloated; there they were out of the incision all over the outside of my belly. I had the thought that they looked just like his red bloated balls and penis. I was sure I could not be put back together again. Then the panic was gone along with the pain. The man with the red-hot balls struggled out of his bed and, holding his genitalia in both hands, left the room. In a few minutes he returned with several people. I was in a semi-stupor. I heard words "dehiscence" and "evisceration." Someone called for hot sterile towels which they covered my intestine with. I didn't feel anything. I coughed a few times, and several of them held on so that my bloated guts wouldn't spring loose any further.

They took me back to the O.R. They had to cut a hole into the intestine to deflate it so it would fit back where it belonged. Later on this iliostomy formed a fistula through the outside skin which took months to heal. My belly was bound tightly so the abdominal muscles wouldn't open the incision. My cough was controlled with drugs and a complicated vaporizer. They were afraid of pneumonia and peritonitis, but I developed neither. I was chastized for not calling the doctor earlier, but I heard an intern whisper that for him it had been a very valuable experience. I had been a good patient after all. When I left I thanked the man with the red-hot balls for saving my life.

SINCE HE GAVE UP baiting the Vaudoise police he no longer visited us as often, so we decided to visit him at his apartment in Geneva. Eating on the train was very pleasant. Swiss timing was perfect, and the train pulled in five minutes after we paid our check.

He responded to our knock on his door almost immediately. "You got me just in time," he said. He wore a sheet with two holes. One for his head and one for his penis which, sheathed in a condom, hung limp through the smaller hole. "You know I have this thing," he said, "I like screwing but I'm afraid of getting contaminated." "You hate women," my wife said. "No," he protested, "I really love them." Then the girl came out of the room, thin, dark, plain looking, and naked. He excused himself and asked us to please wait for him in the kitchen. Arranging his sheet, he led her back to the bedroom.

We waited and said nothing. Twenty minutes later they came out fully dressed. He was affectionate and gentle with her—in fact they were both quite tender and loving with each other. Aside from a few words just barely acknowledging our presence they hardly spoke to us. It soon became apparent that they were about to return to the bedroom, so we said goodbye and left.

We stuffed ourselves with food and wine on the way back

from Geneva. When the waiter brought us klopfers, the Swiss equivalent of large hot dogs, lying on white napkins, we both went into uncontrollable laughing fits. Everyone in the dining car seemed terribly annoyed. Again we paid our checks just five minutes before we arrived.

HE WAS BROUGHT UP on charges of not showering. They called witness after witness. His platoon leader swore that he never showered. He was in trouble from the beginning. We knew he would never be commissioned. He was too short for the navy. His uniform did not fit well. Nobody could understand how he had been admitted to the program in the first place. Somebody said it was because his father was a disabled veteran. But the navy wouldn't admit its mistake. They needed something concrete. Some of his friends called him "the big stink." This was somehow converted to the showering charge. Nobody in charge bothered to research the origin of the title. It started only because he had the habit of saying "the stinking this," "the stinking that." At first I refused to testify, as did our other two roommates, but then we testified after all. We told them he did in fact shower. They commended us for our loyalty but didn't believe us.

We comprised the punishment detail. For two weeks, at four-thirty in the morning, we were to supervise his showering. He was to use only cold water and a floor scrubbing brush. He protested the sentence to the chief of the Bureau of Naval Personnel and was sent to join the fleet as a seaman third class. I met him in the hospital two years later. He was a bosun's mate first class and wore the navy's highest decorations for valor in combat. But he was blind and his face was composed of multi-layered patches of skin grafts. A Very gun had exploded in his hand. He seemed optimistic and glad we met, though he said it was a "stinking war."

. . .

WHEN WE FIRST ARRIVED that winter my French was very poor. I had no idea a trial was going on. Then I met the bookstore man, who spoke English. He told me the trial kept him in a state of considerable agitation. Later on, I found out that one of the six men on trial was from his platoon.

There was much talk in the cafés, on the radio, in the streets. The newspapers were full of the trial. I knew the French words for treason, neutrality, and mobilization and I heard these words repeated many times during those weeks.

The bookstore man told me that the men, all French Swiss, were accused of turning military information over to the Germans. The information contained the plan of the interior devised by the General. If the Germans threatened to invade, mobilization was to take place at once. The entire population was to be moved into the interior, hollowed out, and heavily fortified mountains where a seven-year food supply had been stored. The mountain passes to Austria, France, Italy, and Germany were to be blown up. Swiss troops would harass the enemy. The threat was believed to have sustained Swiss neutrality. The accused men had compromised that neutrality.

The tribunal federal found the men guilty and sentenced them to be shot in the spring. The bookstore man became increasingly agitated. He told me that the law demanded that each man was to be shot by his own platoon. He had already received notice of having to be on one of the firing squads. There was no way out. He told me that he had never shot anybody or anything but targets in his life. By the spring he had lost a great deal of weight and was quite depressed. The Swiss Army doctors refused to relieve him of his assignment. He told me he hardly knew the man but already felt like a murderer. The Swiss had abolished capital punishment years earlier. Treason was the exception.

I left for the summer. When I returned in the fall I could tell immediately that he was no longer depressed. He told me that his conflict had been enormous. He didn't know whether to shoot accurately or to purposely miss. He felt that missing would be unfair to his fellow executioners. He said he aimed as well as possible, and the man seemed to be dead before the platoon leader administered the coup de grâce. I told him that I was glad it was over and that he felt better and had regained the weight he had lost. But he said that it was more than its being over. On my way out he said he could do it again if need be—this time "rather easily." He told me that the whole experience had somehow been uplifting. He didn't know why, but he "confessed" that he felt better for having done it.

I LOVED the secondhand business. The place was warm and there was always hot coffee, rolls, and butter for anyone who wanted them. There was also always a great variety of people, places, and goods.

I remember going to one apartment with him three times in as many months before we caught on that it belonged to another secondhand dealer who disposed of his goods that way. He claimed that he was selling the estate of his dead brother.

We met all kinds of people and bought and turned down all kinds of goods. One of the estate ladies offered herself to both my father and me and I admired the delicacy and respect with which he turned her down. I distinctly remember his saying "No, *but thank you anyway*," several times. In time I also came to believe that my father, through his business, sold poor people things they needed that they couldn't possibly get otherwise. I convinced myself that he was a kind of Robin Hood.

And then I came to hate the secondhand business, though not because some of our relatives hated it. They thought it was demeaning: it made my father a "junk dealer," a "peddler"—he was no longer a pharmacist, a professional man. But this didn't disturb me in the least. For me there was something worse. I blamed the secondhand business for making my father a thief—a petty thief.

There was an organization that collected old suits which they distributed to refugees who were the victims of various wars. They sold surplus suits to dealers every three months and used the money to partially finance their operation. The sales method was very simple: the dealers went up to a huge loft in which there were hundreds of suits. They were assigned clerks and given empty barrels, wheeled about on dollies, which they filled themselves at two dollars per suit.

I was invited to help, and went with my father and his partner after they had been buying from the barrel people for over a year.

Watching them pick the suits was a pretty dull business. But then I noticed that while my father engaged the clerk in conversation, his partner quickly sneaked extra suits into their barrels. Later on I asked my father about this. He told me that the clerk knew and that all the barrel people knew. He said that for some reason to do with their organization the barrel people couldn't charge less than two dollars a suit even though they knew that many of them were utterly worthless, making salable ones more expensive than they should have been. They overlooked taking extra suits as a way of making up for overcharging and getting rid of goods every three months.

It sounded like double talk. From the way he spoke I didn't believe him, but I did believe that he came to believe himself. Frog, who worked for them—told the truth: "In business everything goes." From that point I hated business, especially the secondhand business. I'd go to the store and to sales and things as seldom as possible, and I felt that I had lost something important. My father asked me several times why I was no longer interested, but I couldn't tell him. I just hated the secondhand business, something I didn't think was possible.

SHE SAVED UP for several weeks and then I went with her to buy a whole, fresh, white fish. He took it out of the tank, stabbed it to the board, and hit it over the head with a wooden mallet. She hid her eyes but I looked. He gutted it and cut it up into slices while it still jumped about. Then he wrapped it in newspapers and gave it to us.

When we got home and unwrapped it, the pieces were still quivering. She screamed and told me to throw the whole thing into the garbage. She swore me to secrecy. She felt very ashamed of herself but couldn't help it. She didn't want my father to know. It would aggravate him. Money was very scarce.

"CAN I SIT ON YOUR LAP?"

"No."

"Why not?"

"Why yes?"

"It would feel so good."

"But what about this feeling good? What does physical contact with me represent? What does it bring to mind?"

"Nothing. It's not a mind thing. It's not an analytic thing. It needs no associations to be meaningful. It's worthwhile in itself. It is. It just is!"

"Nothing just is."

"Don't demean it."

"I'm not demeaning it."

"Analyzing it is demeaning it. I want to feel you and I want to feel you feeling me. I want you to want to feel me and to want to feel me feeling you. It's basic stuff. Analyzing it dilutes and demeans it."

"Those wants to feel. Those wishes, what about them? Aren't you curious about where they come from? What they accomplish? What they would accomplish if fulfilled?"

"Not in the least."

THE WEATHER had been bad for days. It snowed intermittently and the temperature remained well below zero. Our barracks were situated on a rocky plain between a great river on one side and a lake on the other. The damp coldness made it impossible to keep warm, and many men suffered from flu and pneumonia. For some reason we were not permitted to go near the town. Each company had its own large hut, and in off hours we played cards sitting close to the large crude fireplaces.

It was a strange place for sailors to be stationed. But the ocean wasn't too far away and we theorized that we were sent there to wait for sailing orders. The commandant was a marine major who, we had been warned, despised sailors. He had been there for more than a year waiting to join a marine battalion. His discipline was very hard, especially for sailors who had no experience with marine discipline. Our first experience came when one of our men who forgot his earmuffs rubbed his ears during a meal formation. We had to stand without moving before the mess hut for fifteen minutes before each meal. The marine major ordered him to the semi-heated brig on bread and water for three days. When the man protested that it was fear of frostbite that prompted his ear rubbing, the major increased his bread and water brig time to five days.

Our second experience came a month after we arrived. It had been snowing all week. I was in the middle of a dream in which I was in a great cold barren place screaming that the navy had forgotten us. I was awakened by the shrill bosun's whistle, the muster signal at four o'clock in the morning.

We lined up in platoon formation in the middle of the barracks square. I realized that all companies had been mustered, the entire station. There were six companies of about a hundred men each.

He barked out that a man had been seen in the town that night and had again been seen sneaking back into the barracks area at two in the morning. He commanded the man to give himself up. No one moved. He marched us to a large snow-covered field close by. Again he commanded the culprit to give himself up and again no one moved. He made us run double time up and back through the field of snow for half an hour. Then we stood in formation, soaking wet, and again he asked for the man to step forward. Still there was no response. He ordered us back to our barracks for ten minutes to talk things over. We used the time to change to dry clothes. Then he had us out in the snow running again. I was soaking wet and my ears were freezing when once again he sent us back inside to talk things over. This time he gave us half an hour.

One man, a thin, tall, quiet fellow from the city, told us he was the one. He felt he had to see some people, some lights, so he went into the town. It turned out to be a small cluster of houses and nothing more—perhaps that's why we weren't permitted to go there. The illusion of a real town nearby gave us some hope. He told us he was going to turn himself in. We immediately divided into two groups, people from big cities and those from small towns, villages, and farms. The country men urged him to do just that, to turn himself in at once, even before the commandant called us out again. The city men urged him to do no such thing. I told him to ride it out and the city men backed me. Somehow, I became spokesman for that group, and a huge, former coal miner known as "Coals" became leader of the rural group. Suddenly we confronted each other and both of us were equally adamant. We started out politely, but in minutes it changed. I felt that my life depended on his not giving himself up. Coals and I screamed at each other. The city men backed me. The others backed him. No one crossed lines. Then, the bosun's whistle blew. The commandant had called us out again.

It was snowing and colder than ever. This time he said nothing. His subordinate ordered us to run. I had the strange thought—what if we refused? What if we all refused? But that was it. That is always it. We couldn't tell each other—much less count on each other—to refuse, and so we ran and the thought of refusal safely disappeared in the full snowstorm that had developed. This time he only kept us out for ten minutes. But duck waddling in the snow was enough to make us freezing wet and miserable. His adjutant ordered us back but told us not to bother drying off unless the man gave himself up.

But after half an hour he still had not called us back. We speculated that it was over. Perhaps we had won. We did dry off, however, and at least half of us remained undressed. The others changed into clean dry uniforms. An hour passed. The snow stopped and it was beginning to get light out, the grey light of that region which most of us would never get used to. We could still sleep for an hour before reveille and some of us went back to bed. Then the bosun's fall out whistle came on the loudspeaker again and his voice told us to "instantly" fall out on the double. And we did, some of us wearing only skivie shorts. This time he did not order us to exercise; we were forced to stand at attention without moving for eight minutes. I had my watch on and I timed it—eight minutes. I had never been so cold before—eight minutes. I could hardly move when he ordered us back.

As soon as we got into the barracks Coals pushed through everyone to me. "Jew bastard!" he screamed at me. We were instantly divided into the two groups. "The fucker doesn't turn himself in I'm going to kill you!" The culprit said in a tired, resigned voice, "I'll do it—I'm turning myself in." I heard myself say, "No you won't!" Coals came to get me. I had my back up against the wall adjacent to the fireplace we used. I grabbed a sharp-edged heavy iron poker and I was determined to kill him. I thought of the drunk in the square in front of my father's store. I thought of the man beating the taxi driver. I thought of my grandfather being pulled off the train and beaten to death. I was going to cut his head off. I knew it. I was going to kill him. But then people from my side pinned me against the wall. People from his side held him fast. The culprit went out the door and gave himself up. At that exact moment six men from the other companies gave themselves up too. The seven men had all been to town without leave.

The seven of them were put in solitary confinement, on bread and water for two weeks. Coals and I managed to avoid each other for the rest of our stay in that place. Then we went on to separate stations.

FROM THE TIME OF THE MONSTER haircut and after he lost the summer job, he became increasingly incompetent and I became responsible for him. At first this shift and development was imperceptible. After several months I was trapped: he was dependent on me and I needed to take care of him. I'm not sure whose needs were greater. There were times I fought with anyone who picked on him and other times when I let them go ahead. But I did little or nothing to enhance their taking him seriously. He became a mascot. There were times he made heroic gestures to be otherwise; to be what he may have been before he met us and particularly me. He'd stand up to us, yell, disagree, but it would last for only a few minutes. Then he'd smile, apologize, shrink, and we knew he was a mascot after all. It was as if we had somehow drained the inner substance of him. More than that we had somehow created a wound from which leaked anything he tried to fill up with. He remained wounded and empty and served as my disciple. Looking back I'm sure I didn't want a disciple, yet I came to need him for a sense of completeness.

It developed that way and both of us were powerless to change it. We were locked into roles of mutual dependency. To everyone we knew, he was dependent on me. My dependency on him remained secret. Years later when he died only I realized that my tears were mainly for myself and because of a kind of status I had lost.

Before he died he spent several weeks in a lunatic asylum. I visited him every day. He sat and stared at a wall, too depressed to talk. Just before he left the hospital, when the doctor said he was "better," he told me that he looked forward to dying. He said that he heard that some people saw death as the "great equalizer" which brought them down from godlike proportions to human ones. He, on the contrary, saw death as raising him up from the inanimate and unhuman to being a "real person." "If I can die, that should be proof that I was not nothing, that I once lived, that I was a person after all."

When he got home he didn't eat. We tried to entice him with all kinds of fancy foods but it didn't work. I knew that Chinese food was his favorite, but he wouldn't touch it. Each time I tried, I was ashamed, not because I failed but because

I had the fantasy of trying to get a pet dog I had as a child to eat. We screamed, pleaded, argued, and blackmailed, too, threatening to abandon him altogether, but he only smiled and slowly wasted away. Perhaps our failure was his revenge or maybe it was the fact that he had become the center of our attention and even in command of us, but as he starved to death he seemed to become more and more content. At first he'd answer us with a word or two. Before he died, a doctor came who force fed him through a tube. From that point he stopped talking but smiled and had a peaceful look all the time. The tube feeding didn't help at all and when he died his expression was almost euphoric. That night I couldn't sleep and thought of him on the bike and roller skates knocking everyone down and I laughed and I cried.

I WALKED THROUGH THE CITY like the kiss of death. On that day I was afflicted with a strange talent. In looking at people's faces, I didn't see them as they actually were but as they would look twenty-five years later. Smooth faces were wrinkled. Bright eyes were dulled. Skin that was drum tight and smooth became mottled, bloated, and hung loose. Old faces became cadavers in various stages of decay and decomposition. I tried to stop but couldn't. At the same time I was convinced of the accuracy of my future vision. Toward evening I tried to see as many faces as possible. I didn't dare look at mirrors or to go home. I glutted myself with strange faces. Then I must have reached a point of saturation. It stopped. I went home. She looked as always. So did I. I never got another attack.

MANY MEN had been lost at sea. It was determined that the largest cause of death was men going down with the ship:

after a ship was hit, men would rush to the upended section but wouldn't jump from it. Somehow they would get paralyzed on the bow or stern and would drown or burn to death as the ship went down. They figured out that it was three things—the height of the ship, the debris in the water, and the oil fire on the surface. One chief petty officer said that it was simply the fact that no one likes to leave home.

They set up an area and staked it out with small boats which would act as rescue parties. A ladder and platform were set up about forty-five feet above deck. All kinds of floating debris and an oil slick were discharged into the water. The idea was to keep one's legs locked together and to jump feet first. "Your feet will spread the garbage and the oil slick, making it safe for the rest of the body." Then we were to clear the area underwater, swimming to one of the rescue boats. All the men were required to undergo this "abandon ship exercise." We talked of nothing else for the week preceding the exercise. On the day the training area was set up at least half the men reported to sick bay with a variety of diverse physical complaints. The most common one was severe diarrhea. But no one was excused—no one, as it turned out, except me.

Early in the exercise it became apparent that many men "froze" on the platform. I was chosen to be the group pusher. I would stand on the platform, reassure the man, tell him how to keep his legs, and push him off. I felt like an executioner, like a belt worker in a processing plant, like the pusher I had been when I worked pushing ice cream pops through the brine tank years earlier. . . . But mostly I felt reprieved.

Before they were "pushed off" the men invariably hated me. Afterwards, they loved me. I was ostracized by those who had not yet jumped and sought out by those who had. They wanted to talk about the accomplishment. Some wanted me to confirm the fact that they did not have to be pushed. Some thanked me. I insisted that no one had to be pushed. This somehow mitigated my feelings of guilt.

I never did see the men who were injured. A few who forgot to keep their legs together were hurt. A few others broke limbs. None were killed. I never did have to jump and was replaced when we left the area. I never found out whether or not the single required rehearsal jump helped when ships actually went down. I never found out if pushers were required for the real thing. In my days as rehearsal pusher about ninety percent of the men needed at least a gentle shove after they had settled themselves into position at the edge of the platform. There were a few men who struggled to hold back but I always managed to push them off, at the same time pleading with them to keep their legs together. After the first day I lashed myself to the platform so that I would not be dragged off.

"IT WAS VERY EMBARRASSING."

"What was?"

"Meeting you that way outside your office."

"I was no longer the doctor?"

"That's right. You were actually a person."

"So were you."

"You were embarrassed, too?"

"Not embarrassed. Different."

"How so?"

"I think it's very complicated."

"I know it is. Is it all pretense? This business of being one thing one place and another somewhere else. All a lot of phony acts?"

"I don't know. Maybe different parts of ourselves, pretense, too, different roles, caught unaware without the office shield or other kinds of camouflage. Many things go into it I'm sure."

"You seemed smaller."

"I felt smaller."

"Now you seem right up to size again."

"Regained my analytic stance. I'm the doctor again."

"I think so. But I like you better the other way—outside."

"More manageable?"

"Yes, I think that's it. The surprise embarrassed me. But there you were, a regular person after all."

I MET HIM at the Japanese restaurant and then introduced him to my father several months later. One night he jumped on the table and announced himself. He didn't really jump but rather gave the impression of jumping, hopping from the floor by suddenly pushing himself up with his very powerful arms. Then he quickly hoisted himself up on the table using his hands and arms. The illusion was one of a fantastic leap. His legs were small, withered pipe stems usually folded up against his body. Even on the table he didn't reach an ordinary man's chest—this despite a husky torso and a very large head. His complexion was bad, a dark pitted skin. He had a warm smile and very small blue eyes, all in all a very ugly man. But I liked him. He spoke that night.

"My name is Laznowski but everyone calls me Frog. I'm a great jumper. Mostly I like to jump on women." He smiled, winked, and leered. But I was the only one who smiled back.

"I make a living. I draw a big crowd. I'm a main attraction. On the boardwalk. The freak show. I'm Frog. Everyone comes to see me. The man who is a frog. That's me. There are signs outside. That's what they say."

I liked him at once. Maybe it was because I always liked frogs. Freaks scared me. I had walked into the freak show once and ran out in a panic. He was an old hand at catching smiles because he picked mine up at once. That's how we became friends. He came over to talk and when my father came to pick me up they met. Somehow after that he spent nearly all of his time off in my father's store. Then we used to eat together in the Japanese restaurant. Sometimes when the weather was very bad the freak show would be closed— the boardwalk was an awful place in the rain and nobody would show up anyway. My father used to close the store in the early evening on those days and we would join Frog in the restaurant. My mother and sister went back to the room.

I remember Frog trying to get my father to stand up and announce who he was. "Just tell your name and say, 'I am a druggist.' Just do that and sit down. It will make you feel good." But my father couldn't do that any more than he could eat the Japanese food. Frog and I ate it and my father would go through a huge bowl of rice and many cups of scalding hot tea.

I remember hurricane weather that year; the freak show was closed for more than a week. Frog was very worried and told my father that the show might close down altogether, and he would be out of work. My father reassured him and said he would always have a job for him, and it came to pass that way. Frog worked for my father in the secondhand business and eventually they died within three days of each other.

THAT MORNING I had an intense craving to see woods and fields. I could no longer stand the city. I drove aimlessly over several bridges until I reached open country, looking for roads that were unfamiliar. I made a conscious effort to get lost.

I finally found myself in woods and fields. I was lost and satisfied. I parked in a little clump of woods on the edge of a large green field on which cows were feeding, and saw a small farmhouse in the distance.

After a few minutes a car drove up and parked some distance away. A man got out of the car. I was hidden by the woods and he couldn't see me. He was middle-aged, portly, and well-dressed. He had the business look in dress and general appearance of men I've seen come out of buildings in the financial sections of large cities. He took a suitcase from the trunk of the car and opened it on the ground. He took a butcher knife, large wooden club, and fur piece from the suitcase. He then took off all of his clothes. He was more than portly. He had a considerable paunch and very thin arms and legs. His breasts were fat and hung midway down his chest. Now he had the fur piece arranged like a loin cloth so that his small penis and dangling testicles were hidden. The butcher knife hung from his left wrist by an attached leather thong and he held the club in his right hand.

He stood still for a few minutes and breathed deeply. Then he let out a kind of war whoop and ran screaming toward one of the cows. The cow barely noticed. When he got to it he was red faced and almost out of breath. Perhaps he was late middle-aged. He was almost bald and I could see that the hair on his chest was white. He hit the cow on the head with the club, using both his arms as one would use an ax. The cow, a skinny rather small specimen, immediately sunk to its knees and then rolled over on its side. He hit it several more blows on the head. The other cows went on nibbling. He then plunged the knife into the cow's throat and must have hit the jugular because blood spurted out all over him. He now whooped repeatedly, plunging the knife in and out of the cow rapidly. He was covered with blood and sweat and breathing very rapidly. He then cut the animal's belly open and tore the viscera out with his hands. He wrapped the steaming intestines around his shoulders and between his legs

and ran back to his car where he fell on his stomach. He
was panting. I could see his back heaving up and down. After
a few minutes he got up and threw the intestines from him.

He blew the horn of the car several short bursts. Now I
saw a man approaching from the direction of the farmhouse.
He was dressed in dungarees and could have been a farmer.
He carried a basin, large pitcher of water and several towels.
When he reached the businessman, they spoke and laughed
as the businessman washed off the blood and dressed in his
business clothes. The farmer put the knife and club back into
the suitcase and into the car trunk. The businessman then
took out his wallet, gave him a few bills, shook hands, got
into his car, and drove off. The farmer took the basin and
the towels back to the house and then returned with a wheel-
barrow for the dead cow and the viscera which he removed
in the direction of the house, whistling a tune I had never
heard as he worked. I returned to the city which I had no
trouble finding, even though I had thought I was lost.

We hadn't heard from him for nearly a year. We tried
calling but the phone had been disconnected. When we arrived at Geneva his landlady told us that he had had a flare-up
of an old case of TB and was advised to go to the mountains
for a few weeks. Since it had been six months since he had
gone to Leysin and she had not heard from him, she rented
the furnished apartment to someone else. She insisted we
take two large suitcases full of his belongings back to Lausanne
with us. Several weeks later we went to Leysin to look for him.

The village of small stores and chalets was situated on a
snow-covered plateau high above the timber line, and his
pension was in a chalet on a still higher plateau. He had a
tiny room attached to a huge terrace from which we could
see snow glaciers, and very rugged snow-covered peaks in

every direction. We spoke over dinner in his pension. Three other outpatient "TB cases" ate with us. They "attended" the sanitarium a quarter way down the mountain once a week.

Our friend had been pronounced cured five months earlier and had not left his plateau since then. He seemed radically changed. He was subdued. I would say peaceful, but a reflective quality slightly diluted his new-found tranquillity. Maybe it had been there all along and was a side of him we had never seen before. He told us that his dinner mates brought books from the library at the sanitarium and he spent most of the day on his terrace reading and thinking. Though it was very cold, the dryness of the air made it comfortable. He told us to keep the suitcases and their contents. I thought he meant temporarily until he returned. But he corrected me and told me that he didn't want them back, to keep what we wanted and to give away the rest. He had no intention of leaving. I thought for the while, but no, he meant he was staying. I suggested he would get bored and change his mind in several weeks or months. He assured me this was not the case. He had the little money he needed to pay for his pension, and there was no point in leaving. This was how he wanted to spend his time. His fellow pension comrades saw nothing inappropriate in his decision, and so we too felt constrained to argue with him. He said something else about *time* which I don't remember, and told us that for two weeks before he left Geneva he refused to carry a watch and gave his landlady his clock. Instead, he drew a clock face in ink on a small white card and attached the card to an elaborate gold watch chain. He wore this "watch" and was amused at the quizzical expressions on people's faces when they asked him the time and he pulled out the card.

We made our goodbyes that evening and slept in the not so grand Grand Hotel on the lower plateau, and left early the next morning.

We didn't open his suitcases for several weeks. When we did we found old clothes, several roles of exposed film, a white sheet with two holes in it, a beautiful white gold ultra thin Audemars Piguet watch, and a white card with a clock's face drawn on it in ink attached to a heavy eighteen carat gold chain.

Several months later we received a card from his landlady in Geneva. She thought we would want to know that he was dead. The police had informed her that he had shot himself in his room in Leysin. He had not left a note.

"I WANT TO LICK YOUR BALLS."

Silence

"I want to tickle them."

Silence

"I want to hold one of them in my mouth."

Silence

"Jesus, don't you respond to anything?"

Silence

"Do you realize I'll never give up?"

Silence

"Do you realize how contrived this process is?"

"Then why do you stay?"

"Because of you."

"How about giving it a serious try?"

"After I win."

"Then it will be too late."

"Then it won't matter."

"You waste so much time."

"Not if I win."

"If you win you lose."

"Analytic cliché."

"But true."

"I'll take my chances."

"What about me and what I want?"

"What do you want?"

"To be your therapist, nothing else."

"Expect me to believe that?"

"Yes."

"I can't. I won't and I believe you don't believe it yourself."

"I'm married."

"Of course. Happily?"

"Yes."

"I know. Many years?"

"Many years."

"A lot of experiences together?"

"A great many."

"I'm glad."

"Yes?"

"That you have a life outside this office."

IT WAS A SPECIAL PRIVILEGE for those of us who had been away a long time: discharge in a foreign port and money to make our way home. I bought tickets on the first passenger ship going back, a luxury liner scheduled to leave a few months after my discharge. I wanted to come home clean of it all, to leave anything left of it in that foreign city. I would use the intervening time to purge myself so I could start clean.

After the last of our fleet left, the food became scarcer each day. A month after my discharge, they cut the rationing coupons in half. I spent almost all of my time scrounging for food. At night I dreamed of the job I had making ice cream pops before the navy.

In the last month people spoke of a black market restaurant in a small adjacent town. I had money but no means of transportation, for public trains and buses had not yet been restored. I felt too weak to walk. What if the rumor turned out to be false? I had to get back in a week for the ship. I walked and arrived in a semi-stupor; I developed a trembling which I couldn't control.

The black market restaurant was a farmer's house. He sold cooked vegetables he had grown, mainly beets and carrots. I stayed in his house and gorged myself for four days. I felt bloated but almost as hungry as before. I had also developed diarrhea which was blood red from the beets; that I was purging myself was my only comforting thought. But now the idea of staying at all seemed like a great insanity. Despite the beets, each time I saw the red stools I was sure I was dying. Then I'd tell myself that even symbolizing getting rid of the last few years was good, and I'd feel better. After four days I went back to the city.

I still had lots of money but now there was no food at all. I thought I might sleep for the remaining two and a half days but I couldn't. The diarrhea was gone but I had constant burning pain in my belly. I had nightmares of the old incision opening up again. Then I heard that the ship was in port.

In the morning I went to the ship line office and pleaded with them, but they told me there was nothing they could do. The ship had to be thoroughly prepared before anyone could go aboard. Also, the boat train would not leave until the morning of embarkation. The port was over five hundred kilometers from the city: embarkation was still three days off. I told them I was sick and hungry, that I was grossly underweight, that I could pay, that if the ship was in port I could somehow hire transportation and get to it, but all this was to no avail. There was nothing they could or would do. I showed them my discharge papers but this, too, had no effect at all. One man half snickered and said something about the war being over.

That night signs warning of bubonic plague went up all over the city. The health authority said that shortage of food had driven rats out of their customary hiding places. The signs told us to stay out of cellars and generally try to avoid rats. I fantasized catching a rat and eating it, and I was so hungry I saw nothing at all wrong with the thought. But I saw no rats.

I decided that the best thing I could do was to lie still, if possible to sleep, so as to conserve energy. But I soon found out that hunger made sleep impossible. I lay on the bed having multiple visions involving starvation fantasies I had read or heard about. I remembered people stranded in deserts, others on mountains, some on vast ice glaciers at the South or North Pole. But I could think of none in busy cities. And yet in the middle of my wretchedness I felt a small spark of something good in this—self-sacrifice, perhaps. Choiceless yes, but sacrifice nevertheless. Withstanding hardship, perhaps, or a purifying burning out.

I lay there and tried to fire up this spark—to bring it to a flame and to burn away my wretchedness. It worked. I felt a glow—real warmth—a sense of well-being. My starvation took on purpose. I was being cleansed, purified, sanctified, prepared for a better life. My stay in this foreign port had purpose after all. The pain in my gut disappeared. I felt elevated, noble, light-headed too, but also stronger. This despite the fact that my hunger persisted. More than that, I now had an appetite—not the craving born of starvation, but the kind of hunger which comes of health and feeling good. It was in my mouth, the desire to taste rather than to absorb, to feel with my mouth, tongue, and throat rather than to fill up an empty abdomen. I thought of licking nipples and this felt good, too. When I stood up, a wave of dizziness and nausea made the whole thing disappear—except for an erection.

The empty feel of myself was back in my stomach and my

mouth was dry and my appetite gone but I had the erection and felt excited. The concentration and consciousness of myself was enormous. As empty as I felt I also felt a super density—weighted down, heavy. I thought of all the chocolate bars we traded. Now I understood their eagerness for chocolate. I understood it in my guts, in my hands, in my toes, and I began to salivate. I was in a rage. It was unfair. There had been a war. We had won. I could have been on one of our own ships. And then I suddenly gave up. I remember it clearly. Rage one moment and deadness the next. I somehow turned myself off.

The next days are as hazy now as they were then. I remember being given four boiled eggs, eating them, and then feeling them stick in my chest and not being able to breathe. I remember going in and out of my room, being dizzy and weak, and sitting in a hotel lobby chair for hours half asleep and half dreaming. The pain must have been gone those last days. Resignation and surrender brought numbness. I'd either live or die, but feeling that it was out of my hands and that there was nothing more I could do or even feel made for almost complete anesthesia. I no longer cared, I had given myself up to forces beyond myself, and entering this state of the "walking dead" may have saved me. Later on I realized that this state was characteristic of so many people in that city at that time and of so many other cities during the war. I think my capacity for starvation increased as soon as I deadened my aliveness.

But on the boat train aliveness and all the pain returned with a vengeance. It must have been the return of hope and anticipation. I looked around, and the others appeared at first the same. The train contained people from all over the continent, people who had papers to leave, to go to my country. No, they didn't look like me. Mine was a short acute debilitation. Theirs was a chronic course of applied starvation, cold, and cruelty. Their eyes showed it. They were dulled, flat dead—even those of the children. On the boat train nobody spoke. Survivors learn to conserve their energy. The train ride took eight or nine hours and there was no food, and the pain I felt again enveloped me completely, no more haze. Immigration and customs processing took place on the train.

Then it was there—the ship, and what a ship—huge, white, lights ablaze. An enormous flag—our flag—draped over the side. Spotlights were focused on all aspects of the ship. A large band played marching tunes and anthems. There were at least half a dozen camera crews shooting pictures of us walking up the gangplank. And then dozens of waiters met us on deck—well-nourished men carrying trays heaped with all kinds of sandwiches and pitchers of milk. No one touched the food. We had to be coaxed. We hung back. It was all too much.

It occurred to me that our forces could have fed the people in the city, could have fed us on the train. The customs men on the train looked well-fed. But they wanted the effect, the full effect of the starving people pouncing on the food. Rage broke my paralysis. I fell on the food and gorged myself and the people closest to me did the same and the people next to them followed suit and we ate and ate and the movie cameras whirled. On the trip back all of us ate and many vomited repeatedly. Some of the passengers were very sick and left the ship by stretcher when we arrived. But there it was again, a band on the dock and more cameras to record the first "luxury" boatload of passengers arriving after the war.

I took a room in the city. I didn't tell them I was back. At first I just wanted to be alone. Then I felt I had no choice. I had to be alone. After a few days I didn't leave the room at all. I had nightmares of still being in the navy and in the foreign city. They wouldn't let me go. I would have to stay forever. In the morning I'd stare at myself in the mirror. In the afternoon I'd ruminate about past events. At night I'd try to think about the future but nothing came, not even about the next day. Then I'd sleep and I was on many stations and foreign places again, and I'd wake up in a sweat and rush to the mirror again.

I started to sleep afternoons, but this too became painful. It was the first three or four minutes after waking up. I'd reach out to emptiness. I'd find myself at an edge at which I could feel nonexistence. I'd be caught between sleep and being awake, and for several minutes I couldn't go either way. This between period was the void, and struggling for full consciousness was necessary to keep from being sucked into it. This was half death, and each day I'd wake and realize that half the day was gone.

One night, I woke up dreaming that a loud voice had called my name and I knew something had changed. I had no urge to look in the mirror. I left some navy things I still had in the closet and went home.

They thought I had just got in from there. I told them I was home for good. My father and I drank and talked until daylight. We were very happy. I went to bed and slept through an entire day and night. The dreams were over. They died in that room with my uniforms. I was finally out and separated. Eventually the whole thing came to feel like a vague dream.

IT's TRUE that it happened long ago. It's true I was very young. It's true that I drank a lot of sake with my friend and his parents before I went on into the restaurant. But I know I didn't dream it. My memory is very good. I know for a fact that the man who managed the place for a short time was a Jewish scholar in oriental studies, that is, a Jew who had several degrees in oriental studies from a major university.

I remember he was the first to speak up that night. Japanese food was cheap and the place was crowded. I sat at a table, dizzy, drinking tea, and waiting for my father to pick me up after he closed the store to take me back to our rooming house. The Jewish manager clapped his hands. I remember he had a thick black beard and wore glasses. "I am a Jew," he announced. "I've only this to say," he went on. "I am a scholar in oriental studies. I manage this place for orientals. I've nothing more to say."

A large fat man got up. "I'm a man," he said. "I think I know what it would feel like to be a woman. I would have a vagina. There would be a clitoris. I can feel it in my mind. I would not like to feel wet stuff dripping out of it. Yet, I suppose this is all theory—since I am a man that gap between my imagination and the reality can never be closed."

A small Japanese man got up—"You are not only a man in your lower part," he said. "You are also a man in your head. You are also a man in each cell of your body. Each cell has a gene on a chromosome which is different than the gene on the same chromosome in each cell of a woman's body. I take elementary biology at night school and I know this is so."

A very tall thin man got up. He glowered at everybody and then sat down saying nothing at all.

A short nondescript man got up and said, "I make fifty thousand dollars a year." He sat down. I sat fairly close to him and heard him say to his wife in a whisper, "I've wanted to tell everyone that for years." "Stupid," she spat back at him. For quite some time everybody ate and it seemed like an ordinary cheap Japanese restaurant again. Then a woman got up. "Look at me," she commanded. We all looked. Her face was badly damaged. There was only a little hole where her mouth should have been—and she had no lips or proper chin. Half her nose was gone and what there was of her face was all white scar tissue. But she spoke clearly and softly and she smoked a cigarette well and I could also see her drink from a sake cup. "It's none of your business how long I've been this way. And it's none of your business how I got this way. You see I do smoke and eat and drink like the rest of you. My forehead is nice. Will someone, anyone come here and kiss me on the forehead?"

The fifty-thousand-dollar-a-year man kissed her on the forehead. Nobody made a sound.

ONE NIGHT, years after my teeth were capped, I woke up feeling very anxious. I couldn't bring to mind what my real teeth had felt like against my tongue. All I got now was the plastic feel, and the feel and taste of solid human enamel was lost. I couldn't bring it back. I started to cry and it woke her. She asked and I told her about it. She told me to taste her teeth and I did. I ran my tongue along the inside part of her teeth and the memory came back. I felt much better—at peace— . and we both went back to sleep.

I dreamed that I sucked her breast. There was a mild pleasant sexual feel to it. But I also felt something deeper and stronger. It was a feeling of well-being—of feeling warm, safe, and good. But then I realized I couldn't remove my mouth. It was stuck to her nipple. I had her nipple between my teeth or it had me and I or it wouldn't let go. The good secure feeling was still there but she said something about "We can't go through life this way, you know." I answered, "I know, I know." But we remained stuck. Then someone was trying to pry us loose. I heard a voice say, "It's those teeth—those plastic teeth," and I woke up.

THE ADOLESCENT FANTASY involved a seduction. She had to be slightly excited and subtly, ever so subtly, so that without her own awareness her excitement would mount to a point where she could not say no but would in fact surrender against her own rational will.

But this is not what happened at all. We were in love. We knew we would marry. We decided to make love. *Decided*—no seduction on my part—rationally, intellectually, and logically *decided*—such a calm decision—and we found a bed.

The calmness didn't last. She became excited and I got frightened. As she became still more excited I got even more frightened. Her breathing became deep and rapid and she bumped her body faster and faster until she reached a point where she seemed to have lost control of it. I was afraid to stop doing what I was doing and afraid to go on, too. This reaction was totally new to me. I was no longer in charge at all. And neither was she. We had somehow released a basic force in her that had a life of its own and overwhelmed both of us, who I now felt were innocent childlike bystanders. In the end my own reaction, complete as it was, was rather weak relative to hers. The whole thing turned out to be foreign to all previously gathered information. I felt grateful and relieved that she returned to her in-charge-of-herself position when it was over. We were home again. The force in her had been pushed back to its dormant state. We were safe again.

Years later these flights of elemental force occurred again and again and they were welcome. But other times—I would be far along the way and she just beginning, when suddenly and unexpectedly she would take me by surprise, gyrating and bumping and grinding with just minimal excitement on her part, enjoying the effect on me. The effect on me? I'd be no longer in charge of the goings on or myself; I'd be off and feel grateful and put down. Gratitude lasts a few minutes. Feeling put down lasts for hours. She seemed happy enough. Why not? She had the power. I was in charge.

Instead, she took over and reversed the balance. She was in charge. But this was not the source of her happiness at all. She was not frustrated, she says. She was never close enough to the end for frustration. "It" felt good and she felt good making me feel good and that time around this was her urge and it made her happy. I believed her. Each time this happened I believed her, and each time it happened I couldn't help but still go on feeling lorded over by her until. Until we were at it again and I would make her come to the end before I did. She was happy then, too—no feeling put down on her part—and I didn't feel I'd lorded it over her. I only felt that I lived up to the standard I set. And in the middle of this foolish, sick, male need, there was love. I knew there was love, too, and I fought to give it up—this sick pride—so that love could be there clean and uncomplicated. But I envied her. My envy? The power she had whenever she chose to use it. Male pride again? Or is it her peace that I envied—her freedom from this kind of pride power play with herself?

"DID YOU FORGET?"
   "What?"
   "How much I really care."
   "Go on."
   "About you. Annoyed?"
   "No."
   "Isn't it possible that it's not all transference?"
   "Yes."
   "Isn't it possible that it's not all chemical?"
   "Chemical?"
   "Quick sexual attraction."
   "Yes."
   "Isn't it possible that I feel honest to God, adult, fully

developed, realistic feelings for you? Do they necessarily have to be childish or neurotic because I'm in this office with you?"

"Yes."

"There, you've admitted it's possible."

"But—"

"Always the buts."

"But the fact is you don't know me. You know nothing at all about me."

"That's your fault, not mine."

"But true nevertheless."

"Not entirely true. Not all of my feelings are displaced from elsewhere. They're not all imaginary. You're not that much of a blackboard or a mirror. But I do want to get to know you. Can't we take a walk or something and talk out of this goddamned office?"

"No."

"Afraid?"

"Maybe."

"It's unfair. Because we met this way I can't ever get to know you. Makes no sense. No sense at all!"

FROG SPENT ALL OF HIS TIME on the shelves. He jumped from shelf to shelf sorting, classifying, storing, and finding things when they were needed. The assortment of secondhand stuff was vast but Frog could track anything down in seconds. It was as if nature expertly designed and programmed him for this one highly specialized job. He spent his spare time napping, eating and gossiping—all from a wide deep shelf just behind the main counter about nine feet up from the floor. I don't remember ever looking down to talk to him.

Most of his gossip was with two very old men who used to spend most of their days hanging around the store. Their conversations were always about sex, and mainly about past and current sexual exploits and the fantastic women involved. Once in a while the men bought or sold one item or another from my father, but he never entered into their conversations with Frog. Other steady "dealers" (traders, customers, and just hangout people) tried to join in now and then but to no avail. Frog and the two old men liked an audience but would admit no other performers.

"Freak! You're a fucking cripple." This, one evening from a middle-aged dealer who had been listening to them for months. "What crazy woman would look at you? You're a fucking midget. Touch your hump and a woman would vomit." He turned to the old men. "You two old pricks haven't gotten it up in years. You're dead and you know it." He turned to Frog to go on but my father screamed to him to get out and to never come back, and he just walked out without saying anything more.

Frog and the old men made some smart remarks calling the dealer "jealous or something." My father went back to unpacking a sealed trunk. But he could hardly do it, his hands were shaking so much. After a while everybody just stopped talking. The old men came around everyday for a few more weeks but there was no more sex talk. My father tried to get them started several times but he was no good at it. After a few weeks the old men stopped coming around and we never saw them again.

SHE WAS THE MOST ELEGANT LADY in our building. She owned a big black poodle whom she kept perfectly clipped. I'd see her in a café now and then—always alone having a café crème and a small pastry. People looked at her to catch the latest style, I suppose, and were attracted, too, by her grace and soft way of moving.

Her husband, also a well-tailored, trim looking man left the building in the late mornings. This was very un-Swiss and we guessed that they were from a different part of Europe. He was obviously considerably older than she but still presented a youthful jaunty appearance.

The young men started to appear the second spring after we arrived. I'd sit and study on the terrace. At first there was one. Then there were two or three. By the end of the summer I'd sometimes count more than a dozen waiting and chatting patiently on her terrace until she called them in one at a time. They were always gone by the early evening and she never failed to greet her husband with much enthusiasm when he arrived home. I could hear the words "cheri" and "Je t'adore" through the open door. He apparently never failed to bring home some small present—a flower, a bottle of wine, chocolates. They always seemed very happy when I saw them strolling in the park or in Ouchy down at the lake.

By the winter the young men were gone. She and her husband must have left on long trips because there were many weeks during which I didn't see them. Each spring for the years that I lived there young men returned—first a few and then more than a dozen. There was never any gossip. I still picture her now and then and she remains my symbol of elegance for that time and place.

EVERYBODY SEEMED SOFT, soft and vulnerable. It came to me that morning that we were all composed of soft tissue. I saw us walking on the street—soft skins, so pliable, so easily wounded, especially in juxtaposition to the hard inflexible structures we build. The buildings, sidewalks, knives, cars, trains, trucks, furniture hard and fixed, and us so soft. How easy to be obliterated in a single impact. I touched my arm, my face, my leg, my belly—spongy, pliable, and so easily hurtable. And yet it wasn't fragility that I felt that day but rather a sense of strangeness for the form in which the human condition somehow came to manifest itself.

By evening a sense of durability returned and the sense of spongy softness disappeared. I somehow turned into an India-rubber man—tough as a solid rubber dog ball or a car tire and with a form appropriate to the world of hard lifeless objects we build and use. And now it occurred to me that hard objects bend and dent and collapse when they are hit hard. I thought of cars colliding and the wrecker's ball banging down a building. We the living, we alone can come up strong against each other—touch and more than touch, even more than grasp each other, squeeze, pull, and grapple, and still come out unscathed or at least unscathed where it shows.

I WAKE UP EARLY and for an hour I look at her. She lies so still and breathes so gently. Her eyelids and lashes are still like small half shells. The first time we ate together—I remember her hand lifting the cup to her mouth following a million years of grace and peace. The same hand and arm brushing her hair—face tilted to one side and then the other, and from the time of her first gesture I knew that I'd wake up in the days ahead and look at her lying there still and breathing gently.

I WOKE UP feeling tight—constricted, superior—what I've come to call my Anglo-Saxon, waspish feel or mood. I felt as if I was on a lofty perch and wanted to come down but didn't know how. I was not a collector of cunts but I decided to look at cunts to try to get back the earthy feel of myself.

Hard to believe the sun was shining outside. The place was semi-dark and the spotlight cut through heavy smoke. The runway ran between two sections of the audience so that you saw either the strippers' backs or fronts. It was a hot night inside, but not far enough into the summer for air conditioning. We all sat in shirt sleeves except for one very dignified old man who wore a seersucker suit complete with a long-sleeved shirt and a bow tie.

Perhaps the man was a professor. He had a small goatee, horn-rimmed eye glasses, and very fine composed features. As we waited for the featured stripper—the star of the show, famous for her huge breasts—he barely looked at the other girls. He seemed tolerant of the rest of the men, their shouts and jeers, but remained like me aloof and bored.

I saw a number of cunts and breasts and unsuccessfully tried to join in the shouts and applause. But I couldn't do it. My waspish mood held me firm and despite myself I felt I had more in common with the professor than the rest of the audience. I just couldn't join them. I remained frozen on my perch—the superior, removed observer, nurturing paralyzing pride—unable to really join in, to let go, to fire off whatever gland is responsible for discharging common earth into the blood. I looked at him and hated him and hated everything intellectual I had ever known. I felt that the two of us did not belong there and served as spoilers to the open good time of the audience. Because, aside from us—by the time the star appeared—the audience had become welded into a single many-headed and shouting, exuberant, alive human creature, and it continued to reject us. We just couldn't be absorbed.

Then she was there—tall, thin, blond, willowy, and quite beautiful. Her breasts were enormous and jutted out at us, tipped by large hard, pink nipples. I could tell why she had become a great star. She had mastered the knack of joining and controlling the audience at the same time. Her breasts helped too, and her willingness to pose, bump, and grind in every position possible so as to give each man maximum view of her pink vagina.

But it was her exuberance and energy that made her famous, and the superior hold she maintained. She was one of them and they were her little boys, and her huge breasts assured them of her ability to nurture them—each and every one of them. Them—not us: the professor and I remained intrepidly separate. Then, on what seemed like an impulse, she invited and helped a dwarfed, crippled, hunchbacked man onto the stage. She got down on her knees and hugged him between her breasts. She kissed his face and his mouth and offered him a nipple which he kissed. The audience remained absolutely silent until she helped him back safely to his seat and then they went wild. They stood up and shouted and applauded and in their way told her how great she was. We, the professor and I, remained immobile. But somewhere just a little deeper than my head I think I felt some tearful feelings welling up. I remembered the fifty-thousand-dollar-a-year man kissing the woman with the lovely forehead.

Then her mood changed. She went backstage and returned with a black bull-whip. She strutted up and down the runway —skin white, silky, exquisite, breasts huge, pointed, and jiggling—snapping the whip a few inches from each man's head. When she got to the professor he stuffed a ten-dollar bill between her foot and high-heeled shoe—the only clothes she wore—and he stood up and got out of his jacket. His white shirt was very thin and he wore no undershirt. I could see his pink skin under the spotlight. He had a small potbelly but comported himself with great dignity.

She motioned him to his seat with a stern finger and he hastened to comply—burlesquing a chastened schoolboy. He put his hands over his eyes and this almost seemed like a prearranged signal because she immediately began to whip him. At first the strokes were light and the audience clapped and laughed. But after a minute she laid them on fast and hard, covering his shoulders, back, and arms. Sweat dripped from her breasts and face, and her whole body went into the effort as she lashed him faster and faster. Now the audience began to shout. "Enough, enough—lay off, lay off." They were no longer one. They were separate individuals again and they turned to each other questioning and protesting. I could see blood seeping through the professor's shirt. A man screamed, "Stop it, stop it," and I saw two men walk out. I felt rage well up in me. I wanted to jump up on the stage, take the whip, and shove it up her ass—no, better yet her cunt. The old man swayed from side to side and moaned gently and she stopped. She threw the whip backstage, got on her back, spread her legs, and showed each half of the audience her open vagina. We all clapped mechanically and she left the stage. As we filed out someone asked the professor if he was all right. "Just fine," he said, "Just fine." "Did it hurt?" someone asked him. "A bit of a sting," he said, "but you get used to it and you can even get to like it, to love it," and then he laughed and so did the rest of us. He seemed more dignified than ever but he had somehow become one of them. I still felt separate but less waspish and a little looser.

I wandered around the streets all day, thinking that getting very tired and hungry would get rid of the tightness. But it didn't work. I couldn't get beyond the half-cure I got at the burlesque show.

At about eleven-thirty I hailed a cab and headed back to my hotel. Just before we reached it we stopped for a light. The driver suddenly shouted, "Man, look at that." I looked. I saw a middle-aged couple walking across the street. He wore a dog collar around his neck. She led him by a leash and yanked it hard every second or so—so that his head jerked.

My earlier half-cure disappeared entirely. I felt tighter and more waspish than ever and slept very poorly that night.

"DO YOU EVER FEEL it would be nice to kiss me?"

"Yes."

"Where?"

"Where?"

"I mean what part of me? My cheek?"

"No."

"Nose?"

"No."

"Some part of my body?"

"No."

"Mouth?"

"Yes."

"Why don't you do it? Better yet let me kiss you."

"No."

"You are annoyed."

"Feel like quitting this?"

"Do you?"

"It's pointless."

"If I quit will you kiss me then? Will you see me?"

"No."

"Then I won't quit unless you fire me."

"Is that what you want?"

"No."

"Maybe it would be best?"

"You can't fire a patient."

"No, but maybe it would be better for you to see someone else."

"No, I think I'm beginning to reach you. Why are you laughing?"

"I'm supposed to reach you."

"You do, believe me you do reach me. Don't get discouraged and please don't fire me. Not yet."

"All right, not yet."

"Now, will you kiss me?"

"No."

"I guess you never will."

"Does that mean you want to leave?"

"Maybe. No. No."

"Angry?"

"No. Yes. No. No."

"I think you are."

"Yes, I am angry."

"Good."

"Good?"

"It's real and you're entitled to feel that way."

"Thanks, but it's gone. My anger—all gone."

THERE WAS A DAY I woke up innocent and vulnerable.

A man kicked a dog and I cried.

A woman pulled a small child along as she walked much too fast for him, and I felt like killing her.

In a supermarket a poorly dressed woman bought some milk and averted her eyes from the meat counter and pulled her child away from the fruit counter. I wanted to destroy the store.

I watched a woman through a fish store window. She fished healthy lobsters from a huge tank and threw them into pots of boiling water. I held back a scream of anguish.

In a restaurant that evening a man tried to sell carnations but he didn't make any sales. He came to a beautiful girl and offered her one—free this time. She refused, too. He tore up the carnations one at a time, pulling the petals apart while tears streamed down his face and mine.

It rained and my heart sank. The sun came out and my heart soared.

I was grateful when the hardened feel of myself returned and I was safe again.

WE WALK IN THE STREET. We buy apples from a fruit stand. We eat them and the juice runs down our faces. We laugh and giggle and feel very young. Two policemen drive up in a patrol car. They speak demeaning words to the apple seller. They give him a summons. They tell him the fine will be twenty-five dollars. His mouth trembles. Tears fill his eyes. He covers the apples and wheels his stand away. Our mood is gone. We feel heavy-hearted and tired. We feel older again. That night I berate myself for not having given the man the twenty-five dollars. We talk about it. She tells me that he would have felt patronized. She tells me that it would not have brought back the mood. She tells me to "accept, accept" —to accept what? To accept moods, events, changes, and little deaths. I try to sleep but I can't. I'm still sorry I didn't give him the twenty-five dollars.

I ATE TOO MUCH FOOD THAT DAY. I couldn't fill up. That night I stuffed myself even more.

We went to a Chinese restaurant with friends. The place was famous for fish dishes and I pressed to order them all. Cantonese lobster, scallops, snails, clams, steamed bass with black bean sauce, shrimp, and three fish dishes the waiter suggested that I had never heard of. Afraid that fish wouldn't quite do it, I ordered chicken and roast pork and ate most of these myself. They ordered vegetables—mixed chinese and broccoli—but couldn't eat them, and so I ate most of these, too. When we left, I was almost too bloated to walk. The gallon of tea I had didn't help, as it was supposed to, at all.

That night I woke at three o'clock choking. A bit of acid from my stomach must have come up and hit my throat which closed tight in reflex defense. I couldn't breathe at all and jumped about the room choking. She pounded me on the back and I could see she was in a panic. I knew nothing would help. Either the reflex would let go and my throat would open up or I'd be dead in a few minutes. Then I thought that perhaps I would faint and this would somehow break the spasm. But I didn't faint and no air would come. I was both frantic and cool. This sounds impossible but it was so. I was frantic for air. Not being able to breathe was a terrible sensation but the idea of dying was acceptable. During my jumping about the room helpless I could think about it and did. I preferred to live but was surprised to realize that I was not afraid of death. Then I pictured the Japanese restaurant of years ago and my throat opened up a trifle. I could hear myself making awful guttural sounds as the first air passed through. Then I pictured the people getting up in the restaurant and telling their stories and my throat was suddenly completely open. I could breathe again—as freely and easily as if the thing didn't happen at all. But I couldn't talk for an hour and felt worn out for days.

HE SEEMED HALF ASLEEP.

"When did it happen?" he asked me.

"What, Pa?"

"When did you become the father and me the son?"

"I don't know."

"It happened and I didn't notice," he sighed.

He fell asleep for a few minutes and woke up somewhat

startled. "I had a dream," he whispered to me. "I dreamed that the old bottles, the ones I made prescriptions from, were asking for me. 'Where did he go,' they asked. 'Why did he leave us!' "

He fell asleep again. Later that night my father died.

I WANTED TO LEAN ON SOMEONE, anyone at all. I felt like a pilot fish looking for a shark. I wanted to let go, to lose myself, to have no will, to be taken care of, to be told what to do, to stay alive but only merely, to stay awake but only merely, to be someone else's disciple, to be utterly dependent, to feel in one giant self-surrendering explosion all the feelings of helplessness, need, and care I've ever struggled to keep hidden from myself. I couldn't do it. Each attempt brought on terrifying attacks of self-loathing. Then I'd try again. I'd come close and feel an attack of panic, dissolution, and would quickly recapture my *in charge* position.

I thought of putting her in charge of me—to act out the role of total robot. This didn't help at all. I soon realized that what I sought had nothing to do with anyone else. I wanted to be a pilot fish without a shark and that wouldn't do. The pilot fish is, after all, a predator himself. Perhaps a tree or a plant, a vegetable that sits and waits for a wind or a rain or human touch but which has nothing whatsoever to do with its own destiny. But the idealizing quality of the trees' independence was not at all what I sought. I looked to feel human dependency and helplessness. Me, a man, a western hemisphere man, I wanted to feel dependency in pure form and to live through it. I wanted to once and for all make myself immune to the hate for self I feel whenever it threatens to poke through to awareness and to once again blackmail me to strive for the *in charge* position. "Come on," I screamed to myself. "Come on—let it come, feel helpless, dependent, passive, ante, ante absolutely the antithesis of machismo and all that it implies—feel it, feel it"—but I couldn't feel it. All that I felt was a willingness to feel it, a desire to get it out into the open like the wish to extract a bad tooth, and I realized that as long as I saw it as a bad tooth—as long as I would continue to hate myself for it—I could not face it in pure form at all, much less accept and live with it and its full conscious impact.

I gradually retreated back to my *in charge* position.

It sticks in my mind. More than that, it brings a nostalgic easy warm and peaceful feeling. I rode a bicycle from one small city to another. There were small villages and wooded areas in between. In the early evening I crossed a wooden bridge and rode into a very small village. An elderly man swept the road in front of the bridge. He said, "Hello," and I stopped and we spoke a few words. He told me that he was the village policeman, but that there was never traffic or anything else to police. We said goodbye and I rode on. This is the scene, the man sweeping in front of the bridge, me on the bike. I stop—we talk. I go on and he continues to sweep. That small village, me on the bike, the bridge, the man—it stays with me and has great value.

Another scene and also warm and peaceful feelings and yet so different. My father has fallen. I come to see him. He is in bed and he reads the Jewish paper. It is winter—early evening. The way he moves his right arm I know that his shoulder is dislocated. I tie his arm tightly to his chest with a scarf. I call a friend of mine who is an orthopedic surgeon. We go to his office and my friend reduces the painful dislocation. My father and I go back. He is in bed again and we drink hot tea. His arm is wrapped very tightly and I help him with his tea.

The third—there are only three of this intensity for these rare feelings, for although there are others, they are not as potent. It snows. It is very cold. I return. She and I cook steaks in the fireplace and sit and warm our bare feet. Then we have cheese and Swiss white wine and fall asleep.

"FINALLY DOING IT. Getting rid of me?"
  "No."
  "You've had it with me?"
  "No."
  "All my questions?"
  "No."
  "Attacks on your privacy?"
  "No."
  "My seductive maneuvers?"
  "No."
  "But you want me to leave?"
  "Yes."
  "You think I'm ready."
  "Yes."
  "All grown up."
  "No."
  "Grown up enough."
  "Yes."
  "Will you miss me?"
  "Yes."
  "Goodbye."

I FOUND THE WATCH when we moved. It was in the box for twenty years. The words Audemars Piguet brought back memories and associations mostly about him, his room in Geneva and later on in Leysin. The watch itself was as elegant as ever—super thin. The Swiss used to call these very thin watches "neuf douziemes." I think it refers to nine twelfths of a centimeter. It still kept perfect time. I wore it and for several days it transformed me.

I was conscious of how I dressed, of how I moved my hands and arms, of whether or not people noticed it. Several of my patients did and several others remarked about an improvement in my clothes. No one attributed any change to the watch itself.

It was during those several days, when the mood of the Audemars was most upon me, that we decided to go back. Nearly twenty years had passed since we had last been to Lausanne and to the casino at Evian. Of course I wore the Audemars, but by the time we left most of its elegance-producing power had worn down. Still it retained something; it was a reminder of things past and made me feel like less of a stranger, and more a voyager returning home.

This feeling of continuum with the place and the past was helped by the fact that so little had changed. The buildings, the trams, the people rushing home on the place St. Francois at noon and again at six, Ouchy, the lake, the steam boats to Evian, the pastry shops and cafés, the same smell of freshly ground coffee on the rue de Bourg. All the same but the faces—not a face that we knew. And the faces we saw were so young—so much younger they seemed, than the faces we knew when we were students there after the war. I suddenly felt old and I wanted to go back—to go home at once to be with people like ourselves, in a place where all people get older. We both started to cry at the same time for the same years gone by and for the people gone; right there standing on the rue de Bourg we cried and could hardly stop. In that moment the watch seemed so strange. It hadn't changed at all. Age did not affect it. It belonged there in Lausanne with the faces that were still so young, and for me it was no longer a link to anything. But we decided to stay long enough to cross the lake and to see the casino at Evian again. To do less than that seemed cowardly, and we told each other that we were not old, only older, and we gorged ourselves on pastry and told ourselves we were fatter but not fat, and we felt better.

The boat to Evian left exactly on time as it always had so many years earlier. The people on it looked the same as then, too: medical students, very old people—mostly roulette system players who meticulously studied their notes for the entire forty-five minutes it took to get there—young engaged couples, addicted gamblers, and women looking for men and men looking for women. The ship dining room was still paneled in beautiful walnut. The open ham sandwiches, white wine, tea and pastry were excellent and Lausanne seen from the shore, lights blinking as distance from it increased, gave us the same warm feeling it always did.

But then on a foolish impulse I struck up a conversation with a group of medical students. They were the same as we had been, full of excitement, love of medicine, Lausanne, all of it. And my depression and loneliness returned and I infected her with it immediately. Our lives had developed along different lines than the Swiss. What were we doing in this strange place? What we were doing was the ancient cliché, but true nevertheless. We were trying to get back a mood, a whole set of feelings we once had or at least thought we had. Instead, we were both feeling like depressed and lonely misfits, and here only after a few days missed home, friends and children, and the last twenty years of the familiar.

But at the casino door the casino host greeted us by name. He actually remembered our name. It was as if we had been there nightly over the years. He insisted we enter without a fee, and a few minutes after we arrived the manager invited us to dinner. The food and wine were as good as we had remembered. We talked of the time we played all night and of the car ride back to Lausanne and for a while our depression lifted. But the place was not the same. The croupiers were much older. The carpeting was worn. The waiters were not as gracious. The women were not dressed as elegantly. The faces were different. I tried baccara and she played roulette. The table and game seemed shoddy. The watch did nothing for me.

On the way out I gave the watch to the casino host. He accepted it graciously but without any show of surprise. On the boat back we decided to leave the next day and we were full of excitement and joy at the prospect of finally going home.

PART III

With Love From New York

THINK my mother started to get angry with me after my father died about ten years ago. At first it was almost imperceptible, but she wasn't subtle for long, and soon other people noticed too. She made overtly hostile remarks, and eventually even deprecated the children whom she always loved. She has been chronically depressed—but in no way senile—since his death, but despite her depression she has continued to sustain her wit and keen perception. She seems much younger than her eighty years to relatives and friends, but her jibes at me and various provocations continue.

At first I thought perhaps she was angry because doctors such as myself somehow didn't keep him alive, but this turned out to be a comfortable and untrue oversimplification. I asked her about it several times, but she refused to admit it. She insisted that she wasn't angry with me and that I continued to be the untarnished apple of her eye. Then I realized that I had almost imperceptibly become increasingly hostile to her, and I wondered about it. Was this an old anger that had somehow surfaced, or had she and I without awareness somehow manipulated each other into this new state of mutual enmity?

What was their relationship like? She was the little girl but also a lackey and a disciple. When they met, she was fourteen and he was twenty-four. He was all knowing, despotic but usually benevolent. They had a strange code. He could say, "Go to hell," but only in English (for them curses only had real meaning in Yiddish, and I never heard him curse anyone but Hitler in Yiddish). She was not permitted to say it in any language. Muttering under her breath was interpreted by him as disrespect, and overt anger toward him as

combined lunacy and insult. Perhaps all this was commonplace among Russian Jews of their generation, but there were
other things too. For example there was the potato soup. My
father used to get potato soup urges and they often occurred
at three or four o'clock in the morning. He'd poke my mother
awake and tell her that he wanted potato soup and then
would go back to sleep until she had it ready. There was
another "game" they played, and I was not aware that this
was a ritual designed to ascertain his independence and her
dependence until years later. Each time he went out the door
she asked when he'd be back. The response was always the
same. "Whenever I get back I'll get back. I don't have to tell
you or anyone else where or when I'm going. I'm a free person!" She always asked and he always responded. Yet his
devotion to her and care and attention were almost limitless.
He wrote beautiful love letters to her when they were parted
for business reasons for any length of time.

But then he died and the games and paradox were over—
but not quite for her. Despite the benevolence, she had in
fact accumulated a great deal of hostility toward him and he
never gave her the chance to express it even in the smallest
way. But I know how the mind plays funny tricks. I think
she has identified me with him and has been trying to use
me to vent her anger. She would also, I think, like me to
enter into their old games, and she almost succeeded in getting
me to do this. But now that I know—or at least think I know
—I will surely avoid his role. I want no part of any sado-
masochistic game, however benevolent or diluted by kindness
and love it may be. I think this will make her angry too, and
expect her to continue to vent her spleen at me as she
peculiarly takes on the role of my father as well as that of
herself.

.   .   .

TONIGHT Ellie and I walked past the spots where the Capital Theater and Lindy's Restaurant used to be. On special occasions years ago, when we had some time off from school, we'd save up, pool our resources, eat at Lindy's, and see some good films at the theater. Those feelings of affluence and well-being were never matched, even though we've become very rich compared to those days. Because aside from the carfare back home we never remained with a cent between us. I remember eating in Lindy's, talking to Ellie, looking out the window at the Broadway crowd, and feeling like the lord of the world. There's no sign of them now—Lindy's, the Capital, or the crowd that largely consists of panhandlers and tourists looking for the lower depths.

I guess like anything else nostalgia has a best and worst. The best is, I think, the richness of the feelings that come back with the memories. Some of those feelings have been gone for years and they never come back in full. In fact perhaps what comes with a memory of the events is really a memory now of the feelings then.

I remember the Duggans man and the chocolate and vanilla iced cupcakes and the raisin nut cakes he sold. I remember the excitement we felt as children when we heard the ring of his small electric trunk. We used to lift the icing in one piece off the cake, dunk the cake in milk, and save the icing for last. I've tried it since and it's nice, but the feelings then and even the memory of the feelings then and the memory of the anticipation on hearing the Duggans man are sweeter than any cake I eat today. I'm sure the warm feelings of childhood make it possible to have warm feelings now; perhaps nostalgia provides the connection between the succeeding nows of our lives. Maybe without it each new now and its sweetness would only be a weak fragment and, lacking the continuum provided by nostalgia, would dissolve without hardly being felt at all. I have seen emotionally deprived people without nostalgia, without the experience of sweet feelings of childhood, and they seem incapable of having these feelings in any form at all now. So I thank the Duggans man for having been there, and the vegetable man and his horse and cart, and the man who fixed umbrellas and sharpened knives, and the trolley car conductors and the ferry captains and the musicians in the park and and and—even though they are all gone now.

But nostalgia can become an obsession which deprecates the here and now of life and even destroys the present. It can help to glorify a malignant swamp of old traps and pitfalls from which extrication may become almost impossible. I have known people who cannot free themselves from old impossible idealizations, emotional contracts, stultified values, and "realities" which exist only in their own minds. I have seen them in states of painful disappointment and depression as they still strive for goals which cannot be realized and which have roots in childhood fantasies. I've seen them in severe depression, still recalling or imagining sweet feelings of the past, refusing to cut those roots and to free themselves to live in the present—still hoping to realize unfulfillable illusions. I've seen them sustaining a monstrous state of being neither then and there nor here and now and refusing to grow up so as to be a real person in the only time we have—the present. Why? Is it because some of them are so frightened of memories of horrendous events that they are afraid to look back and to search out the ones associated with sweet feelings?

A FEW YEARS AGO, shortly after my father died, I saw my nephew wearing my father's watch. My mother had given it to him. Nothing that ever happened up to that point made me so angry at her. No, it was not a simple case of envy or jealousy, and the truth is she was totally innocent of any wrongdoing—but this didn't mitigate my hurt and rage.

When I was very young I always wanted a watch, but a specific kind of watch. It had to be round, stainless steel, waterproof, have a sweep second hand and, above all, be automatic. This meant that it would wind automatically as movement of the wrist took place. But a good watch was no small thing and money was very scarce. Now, when I think back, I realize that money was very scarce from the time I was born right up to the war—World War Two. There were very few presents and those that were given were small and always something of immediate need and use, usually clothes.

But the night before I went into the navy they gave it to me—a watch. It was a round Wittnauer, stainless steel with a sweep second hand, but not waterproof and not automatic. I reacted with great genuine joy, even though I also felt a keen sense of disappointment. It never occurred to me that I would ever own another watch or possibly afford to have more than one at the same time. This was to be for life—this beautiful but non-automatic watch. It was a beautiful watch. I can still see it in my mind's eye now. And it was from them, and even though I was going off the next day we were all very happy. Somehow I felt that the watch came from my father. Maybe I wanted to have it that way, a from-father-to-son kind of thing. But the watch was not automatic and it wasn't waterproof either. Perhaps those were too expensive or, most probably, they just didn't understand those kinds of mechanical complications.

About a year after I was in the navy I passed a hock shop in a small city in northern New York State. There it was in the window—a waterproof, automatic, small round watch. It was Swiss and the name of the brand was Eska. I went in and the man showed it to me. It was exactly what I wanted. He saw my watch and said he would take it in trade with fifteen dollars. I felt so drunk with good fortune I didn't hesitate. We made the swap and I squelched the small anxious feeling that started up in my chest with the rationalization that I would now forever feel that the Eska came from my father. Well, didn't it? I reasoned—since he bought the Wittnauer and the Wittnauer "bought" the Eska, then it did indeed come from him. When the feeling came up again in subsequent months I rationalized further that he would have bought me the Eska in the first place if he could. What possible difference, after all, could it make to him? But as much pleasure as the Eska gave me, and it did, in subsequent years I missed the Wittnauer. When I told them of the swap they couldn't quite conceal their hurt, even though they said that they agreed with me and could see it my way. As time went on I realized that my rationalization hadn't worked at all. I wished I had the Wittnauer. I felt that I had badly cheated myself and had no symbolic gift from my father. The Eska eventually lost meaning for me, and now I don't even know whatever happened to it. Through the years I bought a number of watches, but of course none had the symbolic meaning I continued to crave.

One day many years later I saw a watch in a store window which reminded me of the Wittnauer. It was a very fine Swiss Vacheron Constantine. I bought it and gave it to my father. The night I gave it to him produced much the same reaction in us that occurred on the eve of my leaving for the navy. Even though our roles were reversed, the ritual of symbolic giving between us was re-established and somehow filled the gap which had been there all those years. My father wore that watch (he had never owned a wrist watch before) for the rest of his life. When he died I somehow expected my mother to give it to me. I thought I'd keep it for a while and then give it to one of my sons. But she never asked me about it, I never told her, and it didn't happen that way.

. . .

LAST NIGHT we went to a wedding party. This morning I thought of Freud, who said that if any single dream was analyzed thoroughly we would eventually have a complete analysis of the dreamer. The same thing occurred to me about a party: if we understood enough about parties generally, we'd probably understand the entire story of human relating. Understanding thoroughly the roles of the people at any given party would give us much the same information as Freud's analysis of a dream. But both are impossible. Just questioning people immediately makes them defensive and turns the whole project into a contrivance. But observations are possible however much they incorporate personal bias and projections.

This is a time of costumes and last night there were the exhibitionists. There were Indian princesses, sixty-year-old flappers, Edwardian types, and many, many others. There were people who seemed glad to see each other, others who avoided each other. There were remarks evaluating the bride and groom: "She's not that pretty," "He seems nervous," "Well, both sides have money," "Bought them a co-op on Fifth Avenue," and so on. Some were grateful for being invited, others were envious, others hostile, others happy, others loving, others fawning, others gossipy, patronizing, vindictive, and others there to drink and still others to eat and still others to eat and eat and eat and still others to be loving before others and still others to fight and quibble before others. There were dancers and non-dancers, smilers and weepers, soothsayers and people who remained stony-faced and silent.

But what are parties or "get togethers" about? This one was a ritual, coming-of-age, coming-out kind. But what of other kinds and even these kinds—why do we do it? Why do we go about planning a "get together"? I remember one man

I knew in medical school who was obsessed with planning parties. I think, the man suffered from chronic depression and also had no deep relationships—no real friends—no emotional investments. If there was no party to look forward to he was miserable. But what are they for most of us? I guess it's a great melange: we show off; we gather narcissistic supplies; we establish ourselves in all kinds of competitive hierarchies regarding looks, intelligence, argumentativeness, and so on; we ventilate; we are not alone; we are alone; we let go; we meet; we reject; we feel martyred; we make noise; we manufacture "fun"; we observe. And this last one is where I am, I suspect—an outsider observer. This is not an arrogant superior position I assume; this is the way it is because I cannot do an instant letting-go thing. I've always been an observer and I've always been somewhat of an outsider despite the cover-up, which looks like a gregarious nature. This outsider observer thing goes a long way back. I remember as a child passing people's homes and looking at parties going on through lighted windows and listening to music and laughter and feeling like an outsider even then. Why? How did it happen? I think it was the nomadic existence we lived.

The largest part of my childhood and adolescence was spent in the depression and post-depression era. In those days making a living, existing, surviving meant everything. The concept of vacation meant nothing to the people I knew. As long as it was possible to earn anything at all, working was everything. My father would not close the store as long as there was even the slightest chance that another customer might come in. During those years he worked in various drugstores all winter and ran his own drugstore in Rockaway Beach during the summer. We usually spent seven or eight months of the year in the city and the remaining four or five at the beach. Each time we moved to the beach we gave up the apartment in the city, and we gave up the bungalow or apartment at the beach when we moved back to the city in the late fall. I never completed an academic year nor did I ever start one on time, because I usually arrived in the city a month or more after school had started and left a month or more before it finished. I went to eight elementary schools and two high schools. The result was that in a small way I belonged everywhere, but in a large way I felt that I belonged nowhere. Thus, I think I became an outsider—an observer—largely because this was my actual position. But also there was a kind of superior pride feeling I developed as a means of feeling better about not belonging. And I'm afraid this compensatory mechanism still operates in me because here I am looking at parties rather than letting go and being part of them and not thinking of them at all.

BUT THERE WAS A SUMMER I remember in which I was not an observer. That was the summer we killed flies.

We did a few other things, but not many. Mostly we had a great consciousness of flies and did all kinds of weird things with them, eventually maiming or killing them one way or another. We built little prisons for them out of hollowed out corks and straight pins. We fed them, one wing torn off, to chameleons we bought by mail-order. We attached long pieces of light silk thread to their legs and flew them like kites. We fed them to Siamese fighting fish. We drowned them and then resuscitated them by covering them in table salt.

Most often, we killed them outright and directly with swatters, rolled up newspapers, and hammer-headed sticks devised from stick toys and wooden handles of all kinds. The favorite was long wooden handles of children's sand shovels which were already shaped like hammers. This murder by wood hammer was the hardest to do because the head of the hammer was so small you had to be right on target. I was best at this last kind of instant assassination and also at open hand fast capture, and all this enhanced my prestige a great deal. In fact I think I invented the fly obsession that summer just for that purpose—to make me famous and important among my confreres. Or maybe it was boredom or rage. If it was rage it couldn't be the flies. Surely they didn't bother us that much. Rage displaced from elsewhere? But from where or whom or what?

And who invented hollow cork jails? This was a time too when we made tractors out of notched empty thread spools powered by wound up rubber bands; who invented these? And guns that shot cardboard squares and several kinds of wagons made of carriage wheels and wood crates. Who? None of us, I'm sure, because none of us had any mechanical genius whatsoever. But we knew how to do those things, hollow out corks and put straight pins through them for bars. Maybe these things are handed down genetically, and maybe Carl Gustav Jung and his "racial unconscious" ideas were right after all. Or was it Freud who was right? Was all that fly activity and our easily rationalized anger against those "little disease carrying *bastards*" only sublimated sex frustration after all? Because we were approaching the zenith of our male sex lives. Isn't sixteen the big number the sexologists agree on? We were all a year or two within striking distance that fly-killing summer.

It rained a lot that summer too and we couldn't get over the coincidence of the radio playing the song "Stormy Weather" over and over again. To us, the radio seemed to have a life of its own and it never occurred to us that programs were programed by people, real people like us who also happened to notice regular people things like the weather.

The flies did something for us which was never quite repeated again. What we did we did—no thought, no logic, no words—just being and doing without thinking—pure action. True, the action was cruel and I suppose unusual treatment for creatures smaller than ourselves. But this does not dilute or in any way damage the memory of pure *doing bliss* unhampered by words and thoughts and either conscience or self-consciousness. In the years since then, how I've come to hate those signs on walls and desks which say, THINK. Some day I will distribute ones which say, DO NOT THINK—KILL FLIES! There was no shortage of them and there never is at seashore summer resorts, especially during rainy summers. We had variety too—common houseflies, horseflies, beach flies, and two kinds we called green and blue buzzers. Killing horseflies which are big and beach flies which bite gave us the side benefit of feeling virtuous. But this is not to say that we talked or even thought about it. If anything, it was just a fleeting feeling, and it may not have even been that. We just, I think now, slammed them with extra force and zeal followed by just a bit more satisfaction. Thinking of virtue connected to ridding the world of disease-laden pests was undoubtedly a process that evolved years after that summer. Because the special thing of that summer was the no think part of it, and this was represented and expressed by the pure, plain, uninhibited murder of flies, all kinds, except prisoners. Those kept in cork prisons (never bottles, that was for young children or intellectual specimen collectors) for any length of time were eventually freed. Why? Did we get attached to them? Empathy? Sympathy? Responsibility? What?

Fly summers are for teenagers with still younger minds, not at all retarded but not city sharp. This kind of undiluted, monomaniacal passion that goes on for at least seventy-five days requires a purity of purpose and energetic vitality impossible in a clouded and muddled adult world. And the inventions—prisons out of corks and pins, silk kite strings, food for chameleons, resurrections with table salt—surely represent some genetic transfer from generation to generation, but are strictly limited to ADOLESCENCE ONLY! It must be a gene which blossoms along with other things at adolescence and then dies and withers away when adolescence is over.

Is destruction always part of it? Some kind of Freudian aggression stored up and now let loose through the sublimated assassination of flies. Sad that it was killing—causing death—which linked us to undiluted spontaneity, aliveness, and to full involvement without dilution of any kind of intellectual embroidery. And we were surely "good kids" so it was on flies mostly that we acted out violence.

WE WENT to a different kind of party, a "celebrity party" last night. Actually, it was a relatively small gathering of people who talked and drank and eventually ate dinner at the same table. We had little in common except the fact that nearly everyone there is readily recognizable, if not by face then by name, by the "general public" or "non-celebrity people." Despite a struggle to "enter into" and be "part of," it just doesn't work for me. I continue to be the pseudo insider but a genuine outsider observer.

So what about these people? They are fairly intelligent and I know that a few of them are talented. A few have charisma and charm, and nearly all of them are fairly sophisticated though three of them seem to be rather naive in many so-called worldly matters. Most are fairly narcissistic and veer in their talk and exert gentle pressure to talk about the field through which their notoriety derives. Though just about all of them have been in analysis, I note no particular interest or acumen as regards human behavior, so my own pressure to talk of my field fails. When I think of "non-celebrity people" I know, I note no special difference from these others, other than the aura of celebrity status. The "others" are just as attractive in looks, intellectual ability, general sophistication, and so on. Indeed, they may be more interesting to be with because of their relative lack of narcissism. This makes communication with them in areas other than their specialized fields possible and easier.

There is yet another difference in the "non-celebrity" groups. The celebrity group has contempt for the non-celebrity people. Sometimes it is subtle, sometimes implied, and sometimes it is relatively blatant. But it is there. They speak of "the public," "them," "people" as underlings who are really bores to be avoided in social situations if possible. Indeed, there is an implication that when celebrity status is really adequate, this separation is automatic and somehow removes the celebrity in question to a plane which is so remote from common people that no effort has to be made at separation. Now, I have seen this same kind of contempt, usually very subtle, and the same effort at delineation and separation among doctors who refer to patients as "them." I have seen much of it in my own specialty despite the years of analysis some psychiatrists go through themselves. In the case of doctors I am convinced that the motivating force is fear—fear of illness, fear of madness. If doctors can convince themselves of being a separate species from patients—they then feel safer. What fear motivates celebrities? Perhaps it's the fear that celebrity status, once achieved, will be diluted and eventually even dissolved by contact with common people. And yet it is the public—the non-celebrity people, and only these lowly hordes—who can and do confer celebrity status. Because I am convinced that despite achievements of all kinds, in most cases celebrity status is a chance thing conferred by a chance consensus of non-celebrity people. So there it is—the non-royal confer royalty and the royal despise the non-royal in order to sustain their royalty, which always

retains a rather shaky balance because underneath it all everyone knows the truth of this bit of embroidered contrivance.

But surely patients do their share to sustain the separation
and godlike status of their doctors. This, I suspect, produces
a synthetic comfort derived from a false picture of an omnip-
otent healer. How many people I have known whose worship of doctors is based on the doctor's arrogance and even
downright humiliation of his patients. And perhaps the same
is true of all kinds of "stars" and their sycophants who unwittingly encourage disdain and contempt for themselves.
And then of course both patients and public sometimes turn
on their gods and bring them down to dust with a vengeance
because gods do in fact have clay feet, especially when they
are so human. Sado-masochism always requires the efforts of
both the sadist and the masochist in order to be sustained.
Sado-masochism en masse is probably no exception, however
"soft" this particular variety may be. And sado-masochistic
roles are often reversed without notice and this must be
guarded against at all costs.

MY FATHER, MY FATHER, do we ever get matters settled? Am
I like my mother in this regard? No! Our arguments were
intense and I certainly vented my spleen. When I think of
him—and I do at least several times a day—it's with feelings
of affection and sorrow, because I miss him sorely. I sit outside
the new beach house we just bought and think how much he
would have loved this. The timing of so many things are
wrong, or at least wrong in terms of how and when we would
have liked things to come to fruition. My father loved mountains and ocean and deserts, and I love them also. When I
was a very small boy, before our fights started, he and I used
to go off on trips alone. We had long and detailed conversations about nature, the state of the universe, the human

condition generally, people we knew, and much of what he thought and felt was interlaced with Talmudic philosophy. Though he was not religious, he was a prodigious and brilliant Talmudist, having taught Talmudists himself when he was as young as sixteen years old, and later on helping rabbis— with Talmudic interpretations—who themselves were venerable and respected Talmud students. I remember sitting with him on green hillsides, shelling and eating hard-boiled eggs and ripe tomatoes—a little salt, a swallow of tea, and conversation, much conversation. It was never small talk or child talk of any kind. It was about people and their lives and problems and potential solutions. It was about justice and mercy and compassion. I was only six or seven but we did all this. My father's wisdom and largeness of heart and patience were considerable. And then it changed. We became adversaries and even more than adversaries—antagonists. When? Why?

It happened I think a year or so after that fly summer. For some reason our palship was over. Unresolved oedipal feelings on my part? Anthropological throwback of the old chief being threatened by the young buck? Perhaps true, perhaps not—I have no special feelings which run in that direction. But I do know this—my father was a benevolent despot, a narcissistic expansive man to whom mastery of both situations and other people was no small matter. It was at about this time that my own character structure began to emerge and solidify, and mine in those early preanalytic days was identical to his own. It is a cliché, but we did have what is commonly known as a "personality clash." But I was not a despot. True he is no longer here to defend himself, but we prosecuted the issue at least several times up to about ten years before he died. He said that my complaints were psychiatric nonsense, but then he went on to say that I suffered from "some kind of father complex" which he in no way engendered. What I "suffered from" was strong feelings, opinions, ideas and desires of all kinds, and an overwhelming need not to be anyone's disciple or sycophant, let alone to be inundated. Though we fought incessantly I think the very issue, the continuing issue we fought about—my refusal of his authority over me—was what he admired most in me throughout our lives. I say, "I think," because I never heard it or any other form of actual admiration or approval. But it doesn't matter. There was a powerful bond between us, more than a bond—love—the real stuff, the stuff of openness, tenderness, and intimacy—that was there too in the middle of the fights and certainly in the space and time between these many episodes. But what was it? What is it between some fathers and sons?

I felt that it was his competition with me. He produced an impossible double bind for both of us. He wanted me to develop and evolve, but he did not want me to surpass him. Additionally, my youth was a constant reminder of his aging (now I know how difficult middle age can be). Most of all I represented his own idealized image, which he identified with and at the same time perceived as threatening and a reminder of his own shortcomings. Of course everything about me was less than ideal, and he knew and made much of this, too, but this reality did not mitigate the fighting "game" we were both caught in. I remember my father suffering from particularly strong attacks of arrogance and calling himself "the perfect man." Perfect? Perhaps he was right. He was so full of assets and limitations, benevolence and despotism, compassion and hate, childish foolishness and deep wisdom, fear and courage, and so much evidence of imperfections of all kinds. If being human is being imperfect—and I believe that's what being human is—he actually was a "perfect man." Once his middle age passed and he resigned himself to becoming old, our fights stopped. He died at age eighty-four, and our last dozen years were peaceful and rich in many ways and not unlike the times we spent together when I was a child.

I RECOGNIZED HIM as soon as I started the lecture. My immediate inclination was to stop, leave the podium, and go to him and hug him and shake his hand. But his face, his eyes, indicated otherwise. He looked up at me the same as the rest of the audience—with attention, interest, but no sign of recognition. Maybe I was wrong—it was at least thirty years. Maybe it wasn't he at all. Fred used to dress so neatly—elegantly. This man needed a shave. His clothes looked worn. He looked rumpled—not seedy, rumpled. Had he looked seedy I would have known it wasn't he, but this man somehow conveyed the look of a person who was still trying to look dapper, stylish—maybe it was his tie. His tie was a beautiful colorfully designed rich looking tie—out of keeping with the very worn, creased suit he wore. The tie linked him to the Fred of the past. I focused on the tie throughout the lecture. It brought back the Fred I knew. There was no elegance to the man I saw now—at least he was not succeeding at elegance. He looked tired, worn out, drained. All this went on in my mind as I spoke. It was easy: this was material I had lectured to lay audiences about at least twenty times during the last several years.

Was it really he?

Fred had been part of a group of about a dozen of us in college who "hung around together." He was unusual in several ways. He had a congenital heart condition which limited him greatly. He was very popular both with us and with girls, largely because of his unusually good looks, openness, charm, humor and affability, and independence. He was the only one among us who had his own apartment and who apparently earned money to sustain himself in this unique way: we went to a city college and all of us lived at home. Fred lived in a small but very well furnished apartment and in general displayed a sophistication beyond his years and certainly beyond the rest of us. He also played the piano. Actually, now when I think back to then, I think of Cole Porter who Fred somewhat resembled—and Cole Porter, too had a physical difficulty, I believe with one of his legs. I want to point out that Fred was never patronized in any way because of his infirmity: it was something we paid no attention to at all. Fred, despite the unique way he lived, was himself in no way patronizing to us and suffered from no obvious affectation of any kind. Elegance and the air of the open and charming bon vivant came naturally to him. We did not know what kind of work he did or how he got his money. I think we assumed that he worked for some wealthy branch of his family. No one at the city colleges had access to direct family money or we would not have gone to a free school. Fred was well-known on campus and liked—he provided the polish none of us felt we had and which we only saw in movies. We all knew what we wanted after graduation, and Fred wanted to go on to law school. All of us pledged our future legal lives to him, but once undergraduate school was over I did not see him again. The "crowd" broke up instantly and never re-formed even for brief reunions.

When the lecture was over, before I had the chance to go to him, he made his way to me. I was sure. It was Fred. I reached out to shake his hand and said "Hello, Fred." I was about to embrace him but stopped short because he seemed nonplused that I knew his name. I realized immediately that he did not recognize me. Then he seemed to ignore the fact that I knew his name because he immediately asked me a question about his twenty-year-old daughter who apparently had some emotional difficulties. He called me "Doctor Rubin," and when I answered his questions he responded with "Yes, doctor," and "No, doctor," and all this in an almost reverential manner. I noticed that his cuffs and collar were quite frayed, and from up close I could see large food stains on the beautiful wide tie. I had the crazy notion that I recognized the particular tie from thirty years earlier, but that was impossible! Finally I could no longer resist. I didn't embrace him but I held both his arms and asked, "Fred, don't you remember me—Ted, Ted Rubin?" He asked, "Ted, Ted Rubin who went to study medicine in Switzerland?" "Yes," I said, "that's me." I noticed how flattened his voice was. The wonderful smile was not in evidence at all. But worst of all he seemed to entirely ignore the fact of our ever having known each other. He immediately returned to the subject of his daughter's problems and asked for information regarding possible referrals. I answered him and I called him Fred but he continued to call me "doctor." It made me feel strange. On the way out I asked him where he lived, what kind of work he did, and he told me that he lived in Brooklyn and worked for a hotel equipment firm. He asked me nothing about myself, thanked me, and left.

Why? Did he really know that I was Ted from way back then before I told him, before he came to the lecture? Did I unwittingly patronize or hurt him in some way? Was his not becoming a lawyer and his lack of so-called cultural success too hard to bear? Did he need to keep me on the "doctor pedestal" in order to obliterate the past or to make my advice regarding his daughter worthwhile? Had he been so beaten down by the years that he had to maintain distance in some kind of effort to magically preserve dignity?

A week after this happened I still felt bad—bad about the gap between the Fred I once knew and the depressed man I met a week ago. But it was more than that—it was a sense of failure. I felt that I had somehow missed an opportunity— failed him. How? What do I expect of myself? Should I have somehow done away with the wear and tear of deterioration of the last thirty years? Should I have immediately found a way to restore Fred to the image I would have projected for him for now—a happy, debonair, successful lawyer? And what do I know of his life during these years? Perhaps they were full and rich and alive. Perhaps this is only a difficult but short transition period of some kind he is going through. I must stop this arrogance, this omnipotence. Fred left on the most formal basis, much more formal than the manner of patients who leave after I see them in consultation. He wanted no help other than the information he requested regarding his daughter. But what if I had invited him for a drink or made a date for the future? If only he hadn't kept calling me "doctor." If only he had said "Ted" even once— some semblance of recognition, some small fragment of a bridge to the past would have been there. But in my heart of hearts I know he didn't want that and I must respect his desire.

I AM A SERIOUS PERSON—perhaps much too serious, I sometimes think. As I have said, I wish I could "let go." But sometimes right smack in the middle of my seriousness I am also a showman, a "ham," and these are the times I come closest to "letting go." I say *also* and yet perhaps being a "ham" is also a serious business in its way. Writing, however serious it is, contains at least some of the "here let me show and tell you." But it's more than my writing. I have spoken of giving public lectures, and of course there's radio and television too: reaching out and touching base with people, making contact is very satisfying. Speaking to a live group of people is much more satisfying than television or radio, because of the feedback and, I suspect, the need for narcissistic supplies I spoke of earlier. But this makes the ham thing sound as if it is all pathology, and it's more than that.

I think it is also an effort to open up, to extend one's self beyond one's self, to bridge across to other people and to come away from them and back to one's self enriched with them—with their substance as well as their admiring response. But the line between healthy desire for contact and compulsive need can become pretty faint too, and I think it all crosses over and overlaps in the stimulation one feels when the audience visibly and volubly responds. This makes for a surge of excitement and encouragement to go on and to find still more facets and areas through which to reach out and touch. It also feeds feelings of power, mastery, and omnipotence, and has an addictive quality so that more and more is needed and lack of "it" (audience response or downright adulation) is sorely missed and even makes for depression.

With me it began very early. I can actually trace it to early childhood, and when I was a child show and tell—the game in which the child shows and tells about an object to the class —was not yet used by teachers. In moving from neighborhood to neighborhood I somehow learned early that performing, any kind of performing, was a quick entree into a new gang of kids. It made for rapid acceptance, though it often meant that continued acceptance depended on "continued performances." How did I perform in those days?

I told stories, I invented games, I became a magician, I gave advice, and I discovered oddities and places of all kinds as well as new hobbies, mail order items, and things to collect.

I remember sending for lizards and chameleons, the ball and vase trick, special fast and high flying kites, beebee pump guns, punk guns, magic playing cards, hand puppets, instant seltzer machines, cheap toy cameras, sun picture sets, telescopes, microscopes, and more. I remember buying—largely to show—white mice, turtles, and tortoises.

I remember collecting activities and transferring them from one neighborhood to another, one advantage of moving around a lot. There were baseball cards, collections of yoyos, tops, marbles, presidential pins, stamps, coins, and so on. Yes, there were areas to which I moved, in which I could become an instant hero by instigating an instant craze by simply introducing a collecting activity that I learned elsewhere that fortunately had not hit that particular place yet. I could also be instantly rich in the item in question because I arrived with items already collected. I remember starting a guppy craze in one area, though now it is hard to believe that any area could be so primitive as to await my arrival to tell about tropical fish. Yet I remember the high drama I created in the third or fourth grade when I brought pinhead-sized baby guppies to school in a medicine bottle the size of an eye dropper.

Of course there was that "fly summer," and I'm quite sure it was I who invented the fly obsession, and that one with no help from another neighborhood. I also remember one neighborhood where I "discovered" a miniature forest in which we spent most of the time of the few months I stayed there playing a form of Robin Hood in which I managed to bestow some kind of medals (we collected these too) for imagined acts of heroism.

And there was a newspaper I started—one page, eight copies, and only one issue because it came out only two weeks before we left that area to go back to the beach for "the season." Then there were the stories I told sometimes— multiple serials—several going at one time from day to day. I actually had a schedule. I also ran a penny arcade in which pennies were pitched for prizes. And I gambled too, cutting high cards in a game called banker and broker—and all of it not to "win" in the ordinary sense but to entertain—to win acceptance and admiration.

So, there it was and here it still is—this saying "here I am" and waiting for the "glad to see you" equivalent. Perhaps it sounds melodramatic, but I think I did it to survive. I needed instant roots in each place I came to in order to live and grow, and this was a way of getting them. The habit lingers on; in a way I am still an entertainer. There are always residuals of everything that has preceded.

WE ARE AMONG THE LUCKY ONES because we live here in New York City and still have a small backyard. This morning the weather was fine—sunny and warm—and the air was unusually clean, perhaps mainly because traffic into the city hadn't yet become heavy. I was reading a book about goldfish, mostly skimming pages and looking at beautiful color photographs of the fish, when I noticed some movement on the ground. A very small ant was pulling a twig which was at least ten times more massive than he was. He came to other still larger twigs, leaves, stones, pieces of wood, and he either went around them, under them, or over them. Nothing deterred or discouraged him or visibly slowed him up. He seemed to know exactly where he was going and was going there in what looked like a straight line with single-minded purpose. Indeed, he was the epitome of purpose. The yard is very small—no more than eight by twelve feet—but I realized that it could take a long time for this tiny ant to make it to his destination. I tried to anticipate his journey and looked for ant nests or clusters of ants in advance of his path but could find none. I looked for other random ants but found none of these either. I thought about the twig he carried and what purpose it could possibly serve: This kind of dogged determination surely had a purpose. After about twenty minutes he veered off at a right angle to his original route, and this strengthened my feeling that his journey and project had a definite plan and goal. Perhaps this was an aberrant interpretation on my part but at this point he was no longer merely a random ant to me. I suppose I had already invested him with at least some small degree of human attributes. Again I looked in advance of his route to try to find some evidence of his goal, but there was none. Perhaps he would veer off again later on, heading for some almost microscopic ant city. I watched as long as I could—at least another twenty minutes—but I had very little time to spend. He went on determined as ever, never letting go of his log—because to me that twig had indeed become what it surely must have been to him—a huge log. During this whole time—at least forty minutes—he never rested even once and never hesitated or showed any evidence of doubt as to his task or goal. Now this was despite various barriers and a few crumbs of bread and a dead moth in his path which ants surely regard as good food. He seemed to know exactly where he was going and the importance of getting there without any diversion whatsoever.

Well, before I went back to the office I decided to do it and see what would happen. With the help of a long, fine spoon I held his twig down against the ground so that he couldn't free it. He still didn't abandon it and persisted in trying to free it. After a few mnutes I pulled it free from him and pushed it several feet away. His manner changed radically. He crisscrossed in random circles and then zigzagged up and back crossing his own path several times. I thought that perhaps he was looking for the twig so I retrieved it for him and put it directly in his path. He ran over it, treating it as any other obstacle he had come across earlier. I placed it directly in his path several times and he showed no recognition at all of his former prize or burden. He went around it twice and turned around and went in the opposite direction once. I then flicked the twig away and watched him for several minutes. His movement seemed utterly without purpose, system, or goal as he crisscrossed the same spots chaotically and at random. When I finally left, already ten minutes late for my appointment, his movements seemed to be completely disorganized. His speed was about the same as it had been earlier when he carried the twig, but now he seemed to be going nowhere at all.

As I went to work I wondered, did I free him or did I enslave him or did I doom him to perpetual chaos in freeing him from—from what? From the enslavement of purpose? In any case I intruded on the order of his life and for that I feel a slight twinge of remorse.

MY FATHER WAS OFTEN INTRUSIVE in the largest sense. Not in small things, such as conversations or immediate activities of any kind; he was a rather private person in his own way and liked to sit off by himself thinking and daydreaming for hours at a time. He respected other people's need for this kind of privacy too, and in this regard was the antithesis of the busybody. But this respect did not extend into much larger areas. In these, his benevolence and despotism flourished, and to make the matter more difficult so did his general competence and wisdom, both of which were considerable. He was an extremely intelligent man and also unusually experienced in many matters. The fact is that when he did interfere he usually made matters better for the people involved.

There were the people he convinced to go to medical school and they did and became very good doctors. There were those he helped to start businesses and those he helped to get married, and friendships he started and disastrous relationships and business liaisons he helped to dissolve. He helped people extricate themselves from difficult and dangerous situations of all kinds. I remember one man who was about to go off to fight a war abroad whom my father manipulated into staying home. His comrades were all killed in a matter of weeks. I am sure he meant well and he did well by these people too. And these people were not helpless either. They were not captive to either his benevolence or his despotism. As someone once said, "It takes two to tango." These people made as much of a contribution to whatever relationship they had with my father as he did. Am I defending him? Perhaps. And yet his attempts to intrude on my life and plans was, I suppose, what I resented most. Our life together was by no means all resentments or fights—there were good times too, and also very good and important times, as when we gave each other watches. We gave each other much else of each other too, between fights and even during fights (I know this because bits and pieces of each other's feelings, ideas, opinions, logic, and advice came up in each of us and during conversations between us and other people after the fights were over). So fights did not mean closure to each other. They were often a prelude kind of opening to each other's ideas and influence. Perhaps the fights were necessary to put down the pride that kept us closed. After I yelled at him I was open to his ideas and after he yelled at me he was open to mine, though we were more ready to admit and to accept the yelling than the ideas which passed between us. That we needed this kind of key to our pride closures, this introductory show of strength and self-assertiveness, this antagonistic display before we could make cooperative but nearly secretive exchanges, was a pity and evidence, I think, of our lack of maturity. Competition especially of the "macho" kind is, I think, surely evidence of lack of maturity, however well it is rationalized or disguised.

Of course benevolence is not malevolence, and yet when intrusion is over and done, don't they both have at least some self-aggrandizement as their basic motive? Of course we can argue that the benevolent despot leaves the recipient of his attention in better condition—as compared to the malevolent despot who leaves his victim depleted, if not maimed or dead. But benevolence carried too far must become malevolent. Every psychoanalyst, for example, is well aware of the destructive choking effects of overprotection on children. My father so wanted people to profit from his own experiences, but this kind of profit is extremely limited: too much of it converts the recipient into a puppet without a self. I told him that the mistakes we make because we do not allow ourselves to "profit from the experiences of others" are important, but not nearly as important as the freedom to make these, our own, mistakes. Without this freedom and, of course, the inherent risks involved, we can lose even our lives—we have nothing real to lose because we've developed no real selves or identities of our own. Of course he understood but it must have been very difficult for him because the truth is that he was blessed and cursed with unusual clarity of vision in most matters, unusual generosity, and also the need for mastery which included the need for those he touched to come out well in various endeavors. This last, he recognized and understood least of all, since recognition would have destroyed the benevolent image of himself. The despotic part was too close to malevolence and he wanted no part of it.

We psychoanalysts have to be careful of despotism however, whatever benevolent guise it may come under. Our job is to help the patient to develop in his own right and, if anything, to free him of parasitic and inundating ties with roots in his past. Yet, this is not entirely possible. Something of our own value systems must be conveyed, and inevitably we do "influence" the patient, hopefully in a direction which is good and freeing for him. If we veer too much in the "hands-off" direction, we then succumb to the "mind your

own business" detachment syndrome so prevalent in the
United States. This too can be disastrous, and there are even
cases where the analyst has maintained his observer inter-
preter role to the letter while patients killed themselves. But
it is difficult, all "healthy mediums" are difficult, because both
patient and doctor have their own pasts and residual problems
to contend with. And while a patient may be supersensitive
to what he even remotely feels as coercion, there are others
who constantly and forcibly demand and manipulate for
direction and guidance. And of course there are patients who
want both and contribute to a "damned if you do, damned
if you don't" situation. Parents are only too familiar with this
one, and my father hinted that he too was the victim of this
manipulation on my part. I'm sure he was right at least to
some extent.

WHEN OUR YOUNGEST SON Eugene was sixteen years old he
woke us at four o'clock one morning saying that he was
worried about a hard lump he accidentally found in back of
his upper right thigh. It was there all right. I found a large
well-circumscribed lump lodged fairly deeply into the muscle
tissue. The borders were not completely well delineated; the
upper portion of the mass seemed to flow into the muscle as
if it was part of it. Whatever I knew of tumors flashed
through my mind, including the fact that benign ones are
usually discrete and not continuous with surrounding tissue.
I also thought of Senator Edward Kennedy's son, who lost
his leg because, I believe, of a sarcoma. I examined Eugene's
leg both flexed and relaxed, in a standing and supine position,
but the mass remained the same size. It did seem somewhat
moveable and this was a good sign. Perhaps it was a cyst or
a hematoma, I hoped. But a hematoma would be black and
blue or there would be breaks in the skin—some abrasion—

and there were none. The skin was unblemished, unfortunately. I asked him when he first noticed the lump and he said about an hour earlier and quite by accident. He had no pain. I looked for swollen lymph nodes in the area. I was grateful I could find none. I asked if he remembered hitting himself in any way. No, he had no memory of any kind of trauma. I told him it was probably a bump due to a blow to the muscle, but he didn't remember hitting it. I planned for him to see a friend of mine who is a surgeon as soon as possible. I also reassured Ellie and then tried to sleep but couldn't, much as I tried to reassure myself too. Memories of bits of dire information from medical school popped into consciousness. But I felt fairly well in charge of the situation: I did not sleep but I did not panic either. Eugene came back down to our room about an hour later. He couldn't sleep either. I reassured him and gave him a Valium and he finally fell asleep and slept soundly well into the late morning. In the meantime I called my friend who made an appointment to see him at two o'clock in the afternoon.

If you have managed to sustain a good deal of aliveness in yourself, have relatively few defenses such as the ability to project, to rationalize, to compartmentalize, to repress, to deny reality, to alienate yourself from your feelings, what do you do when the possibility of catastrophe looms? What do you do if confronted with the possibility of having to bear the unbearable with feelings intact so that you feel it all? Is some kind of instant self-deadening or self-delusion, even if they were available and possible, the only answer? I suppose heavy sedation of some kind does produce instant, albeit temporary, removal from unbearable emotional pain. I suppose suicide or alcoholism or chronic insanity, one form of killing one's real self, is a kind of answer. But what kind of answers are these? Isn't there anything else we can do for ourselves while at the same time we keep our feelings fully and intact? Because it is my belief and indeed my life's work that feeling it all fully is the stuff of self. To *feel* is to define self. Of course mutual comfort is no small thing, and some people are comforted by their therapists and others by their churches, priests, rabbis, and work too. But when we turn to ourselves, which we still must do, what then?

I've come to believe that the only thing of value we can muster is dignity. I don't mean synthetic affectation, heroism under fire, stuffy stiff-upper-lip mannerisms. The dignity I speak of is the real thing and is somehow recognizable even in the middle of a widow's or a mother's scream of rage and terrible sorrow. I've seen it and there is no mistaking it. It is as real as any other of the stuff people feel when they still have a capacity to feel and to feel fully.

The real thing is born of the inner sense of self and substance and of the very feelings which produce terror, dread, and pain—because they are so alive in us and can't be muted for "convenience sake" so as to feel only the "happy things." This is not the stuff of false confidence or compliance and resignation either. It can be found in stony silence and also in screams of anguish, and it still retains its characteristics of fortitude and loyalty to self and the gut knowledge that we will fight back as much as possible and go on even if the fight is lost. Because eventually the fight is lost—how can it be otherwise? Is this the "good fight" some people speak of? I don't really know. But I know that dignity born of loyalty to ourselves is the only thing we can really own in these unpredictable and vulnerable lives of ours, in this never-ending consciousness of our mortality, of our finiteness. And consciousness is what I want, full consciousness and full life, no dilution, no deadening; so I suppose the dignity I speak of, the dignity inherent in being human and alive, embodies the epitome of the anti-neurotic stand. It simply refuses to trade aliveness for comfort. Why the word "dignity"? Because we dignify, give importance, to this the human stuff of ourselves in all of our humanity and responsiveness and myriad responses, with respect for self, for life, for its offerings, limits, exigences, and for death too, certainly a function of life without which there is no death.

Perhaps I see dignity as the totality of self, the whole human binding of which each of us is comprised. Or perhaps it is only the reminder of that central kernel of identifying sense of self which we tap and feel, *even*—or better yet *especially*—in anticipation and eventually in the middle of a potential maelstrom.

My friend the surgeon saw Eugene's leg and said that he was certain it was a harmless hematoma, the result of an unnoticed bruise. That night the area above the bump was black and blue, confirming the diagnosis.

SEVERAL YEARS AGO my patient, a previously physically healthy middle-aged man, came in complaining of peculiar abdominal pains and weakness. He was not hypochondriacal and had no history of experiencing anxiety through physical symptoms or complaints. I told him that I thought he ought to see a good internist. He brushed this off lightly and said that he was sure he'd be all right. I insisted we talk more about his symptoms and the more he spoke the more I felt this was more serious than a transient stomach upset or virus. There is always "some kind of virus going around." I then insisted that he see an internist (shades of my father) and he acquiesced but said he had no doctor of his own. I called my internist, a superb physician and a very compassionate down to earth man who agreed to see him the same day. My own "bad feelings" about the symptoms my patient presented were unfortunately justified. My patient turned out to have a carcinoma of the colon. There is no effective medical treatment for this kind of cancer, just as there is no known medical rationale for its birth and existence. I use the term "medical" here as differentiated from "surgical."

Some people feel that cancer is due to a failure in the body's auto-immunological system, in which the body either fails to produce adequate antibodies and defensive cells or the antibodies and cells the body produces become for unknown reasons ineffectual. Some people feel that cancer is actually a kind of viral disease. Interesting how we larger creatures, in order to survive, consume smaller creatures, and that we ourselves are eventually consumed by the smallest creatures of all. Or are they? Scientists do say that there are also organisms that infect the organisms that infect us. In any case the treatment of choice in this kind of illness is surgical excision followed by chemotherapy. I suppose the chemotherapy in effect replaces, to some extent at least, the deficient defense entities which would normally attack the agents of cancer. Surgical treatment of course consists of cutting out the tumor or lesion and repairing the area which has been torn up by this assault. Now, some people feel that surgery, which is a local treatment—that is, localized to the site of the tumor— is a "cure" if spread from that site has not taken place. Others feel that cancer is a generalized illness which does, in fact, represent a failure of the body's defenses and will therefore almost inevitably turn up elsewhere regardless of whether or not there is evidence of spread from the localized site, even if that site is completely excised. Still others feel that any surgical intervention somehow stimulates spread of the malignant process. In any case, surgical excision plus chemotherapy plus radiotherapy (x-ray or radium or cobalt) takes care of all exigences as much as possible in dealing with a condition that we far from fully understand. Some workers feel that an individual's psychology, one's emotional state, may affect the immunological system, but here too we remain essentially in the dark. My patient showed no evidence of increased hopelessness, despair, or anxiety preceding onset of his illness. I've known any number of people who have demonstrated all kinds of "destructive emotional changes" who did not succumb to cancer. On the other hand, I have known any number of people who died of malignancy at the height of their creative powers and when life had most meaning for them.

My patient was "lucky." The offending tumor was removed and there was enough tissue left so that a reconnection of the bowel in the area was possible. Thus he avoided a permanent colostomy, in which a hole in the belly is attached to a bag which must be emptied periodically for the remainder of one's life. His surgery was followed by chemotherapy and he lived fairly comfortably for two more years but finally died of either a spread or a resurgence of the disease, this time in the liver. This time no operation was possible.

I have since come to feel that surgery represents the failure of medicine. I hasten to add, I am not condemning either surgery or medicine. I simply mean that surgery is used mainly (I suppose there are exceptions—broken limbs—though perhaps many of these too could be avoided) in conditions which are not understood medically either in terms of origin, physiology, or process or treatment. It is almost as if surgery is the answer to the physician's frustration. "Since we don't know what else to do, cut it out." I remember as a child the countless mastoidectomies and tonsillectomies that were done. I remember so many children with scars behind their ears. I remember the corrective surgery following polio cases. Much of this is now stuff of the past thanks to medicine's success in these areas. I'm also reminded of the analogy of the fine and intricate Swiss watch that stops going and is hit by a hammer in the hope that this will somehow do the trick. No, I am not against surgery: surgery can save lives and does, and has indeed helped me. I suppose I am against ignorance, and however remedial surgery is—and it often is—it still largely represents to me medical ignorance and failure. As medicine succeeds (and it does and it will succeed more and more), much of surgery will, I suspect, be regarded as that primitive branch of medicine out of a distant dark past.

I must say that my field, psychiatry, also has its surgical equivalents or stopgap procedures. These include surgery itself, the lobotomies and lobectomies, in which either parts of the brain are sliced off or holes are made into that delicate organ. There are also the various shock "treatments" induced by electricity as well as drugs. I recognize my prejudice as regards these modalities, but it is still hard for me to see these expedients as connected to "treatment" of any kind, of that most delicate and intricate of structures we call the human mind. These procedures may be born of a need to "help," but they also seem to be born of frustration and impatience, if not downright anger at patients for resisting progress and not getting well fast enough or at all. I don't feel that way about other areas of surgery and I am well aware of surgery's enormous contribution to both saving and improving life. But even so, a vast number of surgical procedures are proof for me that we still live in medicine's dark age.

TODAY I SAW A MAN walking on Third Avenue who reminded me of my Uncle Benny. He has been dead for a great many years and I don't think of him often. But seeing this man today started me on a chain of associations.

Karen Horney said that people can change and grow, and she meant people of all ages and conditions. I believe this, but the resistance put up against the unfamiliar, in an attempt to avoid what is felt as a threat to one's sense of identity, can be enormous. Sometimes, but very rarely, constructive change takes place spontaneously for no discernible reason. Most times it entails enormous personal struggle. Psychoanalysis can be an important instrument in opening up new facets of one's life, making evolution and development of quiescent aspects of our selves possible. But the resistance to change is usually enormous and often takes place on a totally unconscious level. People who have lived with a *raison d'être* for years are terrified to give it up, especially if their "model" has been successful for them in terms of what our society defines as success. The same "model" or *modus operandi* may be producing inner stagnation and death of spontaneity, enormous boredom, blunted sensibility, and a loss of a real gut desire for life—but giving it up and taking chances with other aspects of self may be too threatening. The "model" is confused with one's "self"—the totality of one's "self"—and loss of the model is seen as a loss of "self" and is felt much, I suppose, as I saw the ant without his burden—lost, chaotic, purposeless, no identifying signposts. Tell people they are not ants, and they say of course they understand this, but many don't and continue to exist in rigid proscribed pathways, terrified of the risks they perceive in germination of untried aspects of self. Sometimes, however, catastrophe changes all that, and the struggle to cling to the culturally condoned pattern is blown away in a matter of minutes. Then there is often either death, deep chronic resignation or living death, or the birth of a different kind of life, full of self-growth, change, and the rebirth of spontaneity.

I have been struggling to get this across to a patient of mine for some time now without success. How can he change? He is a multimillionaire. He earns half a million dollars a year. He is greatly admired by relatives and friends for his dollar success and power. He has achieved the dreams of glory our society fostered in him since early childhood. He is also middle-aged, bored, chronically depressed, and is remarkably unsuccessful in any attempts to spend his money joyfully. He vaguely remembers various interests from the past but can't bring himself to indulge them. He can't try anything new either, unless it is connected to expanding business interests and making still more money. Truth is, he still feels—more than feels, staunchly believes—that money and self-glorification will in some magical way give him immortality after all. And I think this is what it is all about, an attempt to transcend death, to transcend the finite, to transcend the human condition.

The inner laws, the rigidity, the compulsivity, the loss of spontaneity is, as Horney believed, part of a search for glory. But this search is largely part of an attempt to transcend death. Giving up the need to transcend human limitations helps to mobilize human spontaneity. Getting off any of the culturally prescribed routes to godlike status—power, wealth, perfectionism, martyrdom, pure goodness, pure freedom—returns us to spontaneity and the possibility of developing all kinds of new aspects of our selves. But for this to take place humility is necessary, the humility inherent in accepting the human condition with all of its vagueness, confusions, vulnerability, limitations, and death itself. Perhaps this happens with catastrophe for several reasons. It brings us down from the position of self-glorification and godlike status freeing us from the dictates of our godlike or "model" pursuits. It makes time important—and I refer here to the time of our lives. It gives us a taste of death, and we can then effectively tell ourselves that there is no way to transcend death. We can then struggle more effectively to give up magical attempts to transcend death, freeing our time and energy to pursue development of real aspects of our selves.

How does all this connect to my Uncle Benny?

My mother, her parents, her older sisters Diana and Vitcha, and her brother Benny left the small village in Russia they had always lived in when my mother was eight or nine years old. Benny was several years older. It was at a time when the czar's government was drafting Jewish children into the army for a period of at least twenty-five years (It was called drafting but was really more like kidnapping). It was the practice of troops to march into a Jewish village and grab any and all boys who weren't obviously infirm in some way and who were over nine years of age. Many of these boys were never heard from again. Some died soon after "joining the army." Others became absorbed and integrated, losing all connection to former lives and to their Jewish roots. Some who survived became permanent professional soldiers.

Though they lived very well and loved the small village and their home and friends, my grandparents decided to leave in order to save Benny from the army. They walked out one evening, parents and children leaving everything they had always known forever—the house, their possessions, friends, relatives, and the village. My mother recalls vividly how the table was set, with the candles burning, as they had their last meal there and left it—"dishes on the table"—just walked out. And they walked and dodged and struggled halfway across Europe until many months later they crossed the ocean to America. My mother recalls her first contact with New York, which to her seemed "huge, dirty, rough, crowded—I cried for weeks that I wanted to go home." She also recalled helping her father pushing a cart full of different kinds of kitchen things and food which he sold to make a living in those early days. She feels "all right about it now" but she did not as a child, because she still then had old standards and pride. She says that the idea of her father, a fine scholar and sensitive man, pushing a cart on the Lower East Side was almost too much to bear. I wonder now whether or not she repressed any rage at Benny because saving him was what brought her to what she felt as a very painful state of life. I can't, however, remember her expressing anything but love and admiration for her brother.

The years passed and somewhere along the line Benny demonstrated considerable creative and artistic ability. He channeled this into the area of dress designing and eventually went into the dress manufacturing business. He became a tycoon and lived accordingly. But there were ups and downs in his business career. Sometimes he was very rich and other times he was broke. I remember him as always being an open, generous man whose great passions were business, the fashion world, and his wife and daughter. He also liked music. I visited his "shop," a large dress factory, on only one occasion when I had to pick something up for my father. I was concerned that I would not be able to find Benny because the place was so large. My father said that I would have no difficulty finding him. At first I didn't know what he meant but I found out soon enough and found Benny with no difficulty. I heard his voice soon as I entered the factory because he never stopped shouting the entire time I was there. This kind of screaming was the "normal" way people "spoke" in this business, in small part because of factory noise, but largely because of enormous business pressure and all kinds of financial risks involved in the business. As I said, Benny had his ups and precipitous downs.

Things were different at home. My uncle and aunt lived graciously but it was often difficult for Benny to unwind after spending all week at business. We used to go to their house almost every Sunday in those days to listen to music. "We" included my parents, and another relative, Harry, and his wife. We went there because Benny had the best equipment for listening to good music. Harry was a fine cornet player and knew more about music than the others, but we all loved to listen. "Listening" to my father was a full, active, exclusive, and very serious activity. It required dedication and absolutely no interruption of any kind. This seemed to be fairly easy for the others but not for Benny or me. The concerts were from two to three hours duration. I was young and restless but somehow managed in those very early days of my life to commit very few infractions. My father had explained to me that good music—and this was largely chamber music—good food, good games, and the like involved the necessity of initial patience, discipline, struggle, and even discomfort. I believed him. I don't know how Benny felt about it but he just couldn't comply completely even though he seemed to try. He would just forget periodically and make some remark or sound usually relative to the music. I think that sitting still for three hours was too much for him after a week (six days in those days) at his business. I used to be both joyous and frightened at the tirades which followed Benny's interruptions—joyous at the interruption and the chance it gave me to move around and to yawn, and frightened by my father's vilifications. I had not yet entered my rebellious period and looking back now, I think I secretly loved Benny for challenging my father's authority. This "challenge," if it was that at all, was surely unconscious on Benny's part because he sincerely apologized and acquiesced to my father's admonitions and said he just couldn't help himself. My father used to call him "coarse," "vulgar," "a spoiler," "a hooligan," and even "a cultural murderer," as well as some other choice Jewish inventions, and all this in the loudest harshest tones. Benny remained graciously generous and the perfect host throughout, trying to make amends. Very often the concert would "end" with my father leaving in a rage several minutes before a piece was over, swearing we would not return the following week. I say "we" because all of us left with him; we didn't dare stay. Of course we did come back week after week. My father never kept a grudge for long and he really loved Benny. My mother,

I think, suffered genuine pain during those concerts because she knew the inevitable would occur, and I think she took the tirades seriously and also hated to leave. I'm sure she felt torn between her loyalty to her brother and to my father. She would have liked to stay for tea too—tea was an almost ceremonial little party in those days—but she seldom got the chance and would never have dared to stay when the orders came to leave at once!

Then my Uncle Benny had a severe sudden heart attack (aren't heart attacks always sudden?). It happened during the lowest point in his business life: he was broke. For some time his survival was in serious doubt. But he finally recovered. The doctors said that he must never go back to work again because if he did he would die within six months. This happened at a time when nobody we knew had any money at all. The depression was on. But Benny had some luck. He discovered an insurance policy he had all but forgotten about but had kept paid up all those years. It paid sixty dollars a week for as long as he lived and was unable to work. Sixty dollars a week was very little compared to the fortunes Benny had known, but it was a lot of money in those days, and Benny and his family were able to live very well. From my own childish point of view I still thought that my Uncle Benny was very rich. Everyone else said that Benny would surely die. That the sorrow of being "poor" and not being able to go back to rebuild a business, as well as the inactivity, would surely kill him. They were all wrong.

Benny discovered the New York Public Library a few streets from where he lived, shortly after leaving the hospital. He literally lived in that library, spending twelve and more hours a day there for the remaining ten years of his life. A metamorphosis took place! Benny became a great student— a scholar and philosopher. His entire demeanor changed too. He became much quieter, contemplative, patient. There was definitely a newfound dignity. The restlessness was gone. We didn't attend music sessions at his house as frequently as before but when we did, Benny no longer interrupted. His conversations changed too. They no longer had anything to do with money or business. What he said was full of erudition and quite fascinating. He did some writing too, and this was excellent. My father who had always loved him came to respect and admire him: his own Talmudic background made for enormous respect of scholarship. Benny's field of special interest was ancient history. His expertise in this area became enormous. He could have easily filled the chair of any university position in this and related subjects.

But most of all Benny had become a happy man. He wasn't unhappy before, but this was a deeper, more profound and tranquil happiness that spoke of inner peace and development. I remember his being asked, I think by Harry, how he would feel if he could undo the heart attack and be back in the business and the big time and the big money. Benny said that his early years were not without interest and satisfaction but that his later ones involved a new world he never knew existed, "a world of endless fascination." He said that he couldn't even theorize "going back" and that "in the old days" he never knew that such contentment, happiness, and peace existed.

I CALLED MY MOTHER this morning. She was full of complaints. Her only repeated complaint before my father died took place for a few years before his death. She used to say that he didn't talk to her. When I confronted him with this, he said that after so many years there was simply nothing left to talk about.

What does she complain about now? Mostly all kinds of physical complaints occupy our conversation. She was never a hypochondriac when my father was alive. She's been to doctors many times and she is remarkably healthy and intact physically. I remind her of this, and she regards my reassurance of her health as an insult. I get increasingly irritated with her. I think my irritation is mainly due to both my inability to reach her and to her narcissism, her total preoccupation with her physical self. She doesn't seem to care about anything or anyone else in the world. I finally tell her this and now she is doubly angry with me and my insensitivity. She says I have no real appreciation of how it feels to be depressed. But I do. I remind her of my own depressions and that this is an area in which I work best with patients. She hears none of this and tells me about the bitter taste in her mouth and how awful mornings are. This is characteristic of some depressions. I remind myself not to call her mornings, and then I say, "but I should call her in the morning to try to help her." "I must call her more often," I tell myself. "I must see her more often." I ask her again if she would see a therapist. She ignores this and goes on with her complaints, this time including loneliness. I ask her again if she wants to live with us. She again says "No." I ask if she wants a regular companion to live with her. She is even more adamant. I remind myself of how bad she looks, that she doesn't seem to eat enough. Ellie sees her more often than I do. When we see her she starts out badly as on the phone but then brightens up and after a short while looks better too. Visiting her is better, I tell myself. She is not as hostile as on the phone. Yes, I promise her and myself, I will see her soon. After I get off the phone I feel depleted. I'm not a youngster myself I tell myself. I'm a middle-aged man. She wears me out. But I also ask myself, "Why can't I have as much compassion for her as I have for patients?" I know how bad she feels.

Perhaps being middle-aged is what makes it so difficult. This seeing one's parent getting "very old" is no easy matter.

I have caught denial of her getting old in myself several times. Despite how bad she looks at times she "seems" much younger than she is, *to me*. I'm sure this is a form of denial of my own aging process.

She suddenly felt much better some six months ago and there was no discernible reason for it. Nothing happened, no great change in her life in any way, no discernible resolution of any kind of struggle, and no explanation that she could give. She was not her "old self" again: she was better than ever before. She was happier, more vital, more self-assertive, with no hostility, masked, muted or otherwise. She said she never felt so good before. Perhaps having felt the flow of anger for some time preceding this reaction made her "feeling better than ever in the past" possible. But I knew that it was only a short reaction and wouldn't last. She knew it too and told me so. Whatever required change in her for this to happen revealed possibilities for a brief time—about two weeks—and then pulled back again. Why? How? What? I don't know. I do know that it reminded me of our old-time relationship, of her love, esteem of me, devotion and care. She was never exploitative and despite deep concern for me had never been manipulative, overprotective, or in any way stifling.

So I describe the perfect mother? No: she was exasperating in her compliance to my father and was not protective of me in the early days of our fights. I suppose she exasperated him, too, in her complete abandonment of herself in favor of him. This was certainly a form of glorious martyrdom for her. I am sure he would have been happier if she had dared fight back at times. Maybe that too was what our fights were about. I fought back for her. But if this was true I doubt that it was in the oedipal sense of winning her from him. It would be more in the form of attaining my own glory in defending the weak against the strong. However in this case the "weak," my mother, either stood by in anguish or if she showed any subtle evidence of taking sides at all it was with him, however unjustified that stand might be. Do I neglect her now for what I perceived as a lack of loyalty to me then? I doubt it. My neglect now is pure self-protection because since that time I have learned that the "weak" are not always weak at all, and that compliancy and masochism and martyrdom are among the most powerful of manipulative weapons, as well as means to self-glorification. The reputation of the power people wield who know how to generate guilt remains intact. My friend Louis DeRosis, a fine psychoanalyst, points out that Christ's major and sustained power lies mainly in his martyrdom rather than in his omnipotence or miracles. People believe, people will fight and people will kill for his suffering, and the lesson has not been lost on so many others of us. In any case, my mother goes on, self-martyred, enraged, and depressed and unwilling to have professional help.

I know that she has the dignity I spoke of earlier: I've seen flashes of it, but there is nothing I can do to bring it to fruition now. Yet it was powerful stuff in her. I still recall her capacity for uncomplaining work during very difficult times. I also remember her unstinting care, devotion, and the enormous energy—more than that, vitality and life—which she applied when any of us were sick, sometimes very sick. But now she cannot muster any of it in her own behalf. This is characteristic of chronic depression. If only some of the energy used in complaining could be converted to motivation to seek help. When I pin her down, she says she is too old, hopeless, that there is nothing left. I believe none of this. I believe her martyrdom has reached malignant proportions. She has reached the ultimate in terms of her neurotic need to hate and efface herself and is reluctant to relinquish this stand. Yes, she is caught in a pride stand, pride in feeling as down and out as she does, pride in ultimate helplessness and hopelessness, and she cannot free herself from this pride lock. Despite any kind of explanations, and she is very bright, she understands none of this. Her resistance to understanding or changing reigns supreme.

Today I read in the *New York Times* that Marc Chagall is celebrating his ninetieth birthday. And he is celebrating in good health, in fine spirits, and involved in doing fine work. I think of the old people I see behind windows in New York in the winter, looking out on cold grey streets, waiting—waiting. I see some of them leaning out the windows in the summertime—waiting. I went to a "golden age center" and I saw them shuffling around a dance floor and playing bingo and they still seem to be waiting. What about Chagall, Picasso, Stokowski, Shaw—is it their creative genius which makes life for them different and nullifies malignant resignation? I think of Chagall and I picture the charming village on the Côte d'Azur he lives in and the gentle climate and the clean warm air and the mountains and sea always close by, and I think of the work he does and the constant and reliable sense of importance he must have generating from inside, from a self which is at least in large part truly realized. And also the admiration from the outside, the endless flow of narcissistic supplies, how different from the waiting old people I see in the windows.

THE AD IN THE PAPER described exactly the boat we were looking for, and at the right price too: a seventeen-foot fishing boat with a 115 horsepower outboard motor, two years old and "seldom used," thirty-five hundred dollars. We'd been looking for some time now without success so we were reasonably excited.

The boat turned out to be just as the ad described, no hitches of any kind. We spent several hours with the man selling the boat, in order to make necessary arrangements for transfer of ownership and delivery.

This man was about forty years old and a rather open person. He worked for the telephone company as a computer expert. When I showed interest he went on to tell me something of his life. I've come to learn the truth of this—that many people will tell about themselves if real interest in knowing and understanding is demonstrated. Genuine interest, which is the earliest step in involvement, is often followed by a dropping off of suspicion or any paranoia which may exist, and followed by openness and a willingness and even a desire to share information about one's life.

He told me about his work, his early background in New York, his wife and children, and his love of boats. He was selling this boat because his children were no longer interested in boats and so he had already bought a smaller one just for his own use. This man's life as it turned out has been full of tragedy. One of his children had died several years earlier, another child developed a very rare malignancy but was successfully operated on. His wife had recently sustained successful surgery following a cerebral vascular accident due to a cerebral aneurism. At about the same time he injured his back in a bad car accident. But there were good and rich aspects too. He liked his work. His son who survived cancer had developed into a healthy young man who was currently working as a lifeguard. His sixteen-year-old daughter, a charming and beautiful girl whom we met, was a fine athelete, one of the best women runners in the county. Another younger son was doing well in school, and my friend's wife (and at this point doesn't at least some friendship enter into our relationship?) was doing well following her surgery, showing no evidence of seizure activity, a common postoperative complication in these kinds of cases. He was well in touch with the struggles and pain he had endured through the years but there were no signs at all of a sense of martyrdom, hopelessness, or any Job-like identification. Quite the contrary, he seemed to be full of the richness of life and told me that he considered himself a fortunate person in many ways. I have to suppose that his expectations of life are either realistic or minimal. I think they are realistic because this man showed no discernible evidence of bitterness, tightness, having been dried out and shrunk down, or lifeless resignation which often accompanies minimal or no expectations at all. No, this man certainly did not relish tragedy but his vitality was apparent. I told him something of myself, my family and my own life, so there was some exchange, but not nearly as much as he told me. The habit of being a professional listener and gatherer of human information is not easily surrendered.

We made our deal for the price he asked for in the paper. I know that he would have quickly acquiesced to an "offer" of a few hundred dollars less. But I had a strong desire, more than that, a strong need not to bargain him down in any way —just to go on to give him the asked-for price, which was fair.

I thought about this later on because I have made many such "deals" before and there is always at least some bargaining.

1. Did I do it out of some kind of patronizing motive— because this man earns much less than I do? No. I have no feeling of any kind for this one.

2. Did I do it because the price was so eminently fair? No. The price was fair but not remarkably low.

3. Did I do it because the man has endured so much suffering—out of pity? No, I don't pity him. He is in no way a pitiful man. I empathize with him, but empathy would not stop me from bargaining.

4. Is it because our relationship was not "pure business" and quickly turned at least to the beginnings of friendship?

No and yes. This was not my prime motive, but later on I realized that it contributed or gave helpful ambiance to my motive.

5. Was it a question of self-effacement on my part? No, it was neither self-effacement or grandiosity. I am nearly always assertive in this kind of transaction and I know the value of a dollar. Though the few hundred dollars would in no way change my life, I could always use it for something or other.

Then what was it, because this kind of urge, or even need, to not bargain is rare indeed. I think, more than that, I know, it was the need to not score, to not win, to not come out ahead in any way! It was the need to make a symbolic gesture, however small, for myself against years of cultural training to compete, to get the better of the next guy, to be in an adversary or—even worse—an antagonistic duel. It was the need to make a symbolic gesture for myself, to make an exchange with another human being, which would be the antithesis of all previous experiences involved with scoring vindictive triumphs. It was an anti-macho stand, a stand against the compelling need our society brainwashes in us, to do better, to be better, to best the other guy. Our beginnings of friendship, and I suppose also the fair price of the boat, helped me to be friend enough to myself to listen to myself so that I could hear my need and to do accordingly. *Because* this small symbolic gesture is for *me!*

I WAS WALKING on upper Madison Avenue wondering how the shopkeepers manage to pay those enormous rents, because all those small stores were empty of customers and seemed to carry much the same items. I'm sure there must be subtle differences though, especially in the clothes. I suspect that I'm relatively blind in discerning many of the subtleties involved especially in women's clothes, though I do know what I do and don't like. The women, the children, everybody walking on this street today looked cool, beautiful, and elegant. And suddenly it was all disturbed, a small boy was angrily hitting his mother while tears streamed down his cheeks. His young and beautiful mother tried to stop him with words, first quietly then more loudly, first gently then sternly, but all to no avail. She put her arms around him, dabbed his tears with a silk handkerchief, kissed him, and again was back to soothing tones but he flailed out and kicked and hit and a few blows were strong and, I suspect, painful, landing on her stomach the way they did. I could see he was too far into it and couldn't stop even if he really did want and appreciate her warmth and obvious love.

I think that children strike out at their parents this way only when they are embarrassed. Anger of frustration, of loss, of physical hurt, of pain, seldom produces this kind of physical acting out. I have seen children and those not so young, too, hit a wall and hurt themselves out of sorrow or frustration—but this is something else. But anger due to hurt pride resulting in embarrassment or humiliation sometimes makes even the usually "good" and appropriately well-behaved child strike out physically at a loved and respected mother or father. What is it about embarrassment and hurt pride which makes it different? The flood gates of self-hate are opened, and this self-hate is too much to bear and must be relieved at once, usually at the supposed perpetrator. It must be that young children already have the beginnings of a glorified image of themselves, falls from which produce self-hate and projected rage at others. Of course hurt-pride reactions in adults are all too common. They sometimes lead to murder, mass-murder, and even to war in the name of national pride in which the national image must be upheld at any cost.

Perhaps rage at a parent is particularly strong in a small

child in this circumstance because here is the protector herself causing the largest pain of all, embarrassment. And in
a way the child more than expresses rage. He also "gets even,"
and I've heard young children shout and scream this expression even as they strike out. They "get even" because the
parent in these episodes usually gets embarrassed too. Of
course this can be very dangerous and I think that some
parents, who start to hit back and then become embarrassed
by lack of control (of selves and child) in front of a group of
onlookers, sometimes lose control completely and in a blind
rage inflict great bodily damage. Later on there is regret and
sorrow and the whole event seems inexplicable to them. I
watched this episode on the street while looking at a store
window, too, in an effort to not in any way contribute to a
situation of embarrassment. The young mother was very
flushed, visibly upset, and apologized to a storekeeper who
came out to see what was going on. But she remained cool,
and about ten minutes after the episode started the child
seemed much calmer and they both walked uptown. I wondered what started the whole thing in the first place.

I SUPPOSE we all take on superstitions and mildly phobic feelings about things, places, ideas, and most of the time the
origin of these feelings remains a mystery. Sometimes the
cause reveals itself; this happens occasionally in psychoanalysis. Not that the special feeling about "the thing" goes
away—in some cases it does and sometimes it doesn't. A
sensitivity or kind of wariness may continue all one's life
because the habit of this reaction to the feared thing, the
"emotional allergen," has been there for so long.

There are a few places which I avoid even though I know
why I don't like them. One reminds me of very hard financial
times and worry in my family. Another reminds me of a period

of severe emotional depression I suffered, because that is where I lived when it took place. I don't feel phobic about these areas, but the associations and some concomitant feelings reminiscent of the anxious and depressed feelings of those times never fail to take place there. So it is appropriate that those places are on my personal list of psychological or "emotional allergens."

There are some "emotional allergens" which, like physical allergens, affect us, and of whose existence we know nothing. Sometimes we know we are in their presence only by a kind of special disquietude or uneasiness we feel. This can of course go on without our even knowing that we are encountering an emotional allergen. Sometimes this takes the form of a mysterious déjà vu experience, and sometimes the mystery is finally revealed. The ability to loosely and freely associate is very helpful when trying to pinpoint the allergen. I remember feeling an uneasiness on and off for years without knowing why. I finally pinpointed it to two women friends whom we knew and saw infrequently. I then realized I had the same sensation, but only now and then, with a new woman patient of mine. Then one day I realized what it was: it was a perfume the three women used. This was the allergen. Soon after my realization I became aware through free associations back to the past that this allergen was connected to my sister who used this scent continuously during a very unhappy summer for my family many years earlier. The scent still bothers me, but its effect has been diluted to a large degree.

For me the number 2 has long been an emotional allergen, and for years I was aware of this but didn't know why. This feeling about a number is not unusual. A great many people have "lucky" numbers and "unlucky" numbers and many believe in mild forms of numerology too, "things happen in threes," and so on. But for me the number 2 is not that, exactly—the superstition is more subtle, but it used to be very strong. The number 2 was just better avoided when possible.

I was not obsessed by the mystery of my queasiness involving the number 2, but for years I'd explore possibilities every now and then, but without a clue. Intellectual interpretations, however logical they may be, if they are false are perceived as such at once. The real thing produces an unmistakable gut click so there is no question to validity. I explored, had my associations, theorized logically, and had no gut click as I continued to avoid number 2.

Then one day it came to me. I *knew* I had hit it and this was one of the times in which hitting it removed the onus dramatically, completely and at once—further corroboration of validation! When I hit it I was surprised that it had taken so long. *It was so obvious.* But this is usually the case with emotional allergens. We see how obvious they would have been had they been revealed, but revelation is what eludes us, or more realistically we elude it. As with so much we repress, emotional allergens are no exception—we avoid them and one of the ways we avoid them is to shun the symbols which have come to represent them, as with the perfume which had become the symbolic representation of a bad time in my life. The bad time was the allergen and what I avoided was the perfume or reminder of that time. The perfume was painful and the bad time was even more painful to remember but remembering it is the only way to be free of it. I suppose in microcosm this tells the story of what the psychoanalytic process or "treatment" is really all about, exposure of all those repressed, avoided aspects of self in the especially hard times of our lives. The difficulty of finding the offending allergen is directly proportional to the pain which was involved at the time of repression. It is simply a question of burying that which is most painful most deeply, and sometimes the job is done "too well" so that exposure is very difficult. Some allergens don't produce symbols at all because they have been so painful that they have to have been buried completely, and these can never be exposed even though they go on making us feel insecure and more than usually vulnerable all of our lives.

The number 2 was of the more painful kinds, and therefore one of the more difficult ones to find the root cause of, but it was "findable" after all.

When I was a child, classes in New York City public elementary schools were designated by the year, the semester (the first half year or fall semester, and the second half year or spring semester), and the scholastic quality of the class. The first large number designated the year. The letter that followed, either A or B, designated the semester, and the small all-important number which came last told whether you were in a "quick" or a "slow" class. There were always four classes or sections to each grade. The small "1" always designated the "quickest class" and from the teachers, parents, and pupils real point of view the brightest pupils, who would go on to be good in high school and would go on to college and perhaps the professions. These "1" classes were the closest equivalent to gifted children classes which some schools have today. The "1" class always got more interesting and advanced work. They were the most privileged and generally indulged children in the school. They led the various clubs, appeared in the plays, and enjoyed the attention of teachers who felt privileged to teach them. The "3" class consisted of children who were runners up to the "1" class and who were in contention for class "1." Some sometimes made it but not often. It was very hard to go from one status to another, and children tended to be pegged very early and to be stuck with the particular classification they fell into as early as the first or second of eight years of elementary school. The "3" class was respectably viewed and relatively privileged too. The "4" class consisted of a mixture of problem children, transfers from other schools, children of immigrant parents who did not know English, and children who tended to be "slow." Few were contenders for the "3" class and even fewer ever made it. The feeling about the "4" class, however subtle or unexpressed in so many words, was that of not really belonging, of being outsiders or borderline misfits of some kind. The "2" class—and why the number 2 was chosen for this group I don't know—without any euphemism like "slow," was thought of as the dumb class. Academic minds, those of training school graduate elementary school teachers of that time, were not terribly open to subtleties between children who had emotional problems, family problems, and low IQ's. This was usually considered the hopeless group and little was done to stimulate them, though efforts were made to teach them the rudimentary ABC's. The "2" class were contenders for nothing, though on occasion a "2" class student moved up to the "4" class and very rarely to a "3" class. When this happened it was due to either an extremely rare, more highly evolved than usual, and interested teacher, or to the pressures of a parent. The latter was almost nonexistent because most parents of children in the "2" class were immigrants who did not understand the discriminating niceties of this kind of vicious, discriminatory grading system, or were too intimidated by authority of any kind to speak up in any way. This was a time when teachers were royalty and principals were absolute gods. Children in the "2" class were strictly lower-class and virtually pariahs, and therefore it was not unusual for them to fulfill the prophecies made for them. They sometimes formed rebellious gangs. They were troublemakers. They were truants. They smoked, a crime in those school days. They were unmanageable. Mainly, they were without prestige or power of any kind and this often extended from school to their neighborhoods and to home. Most of them,

if they had problems to begin with, wound up with still
larger problems because of destruction of their self-esteem
promoted by this caste system.

To recapitulate, $4A_3$ meant the fourth year, the first semester of the year, and the all important subscript "3" meant
almost privileged; $8B_2$ meant the eight or last year, the spring
semester, and the little "2" meant the dumb class. Graduation from the 8B, which was when graduation normally took
place, was taken very seriously in those days. Each diploma—
elementary, high school, college—was seen as a very weighty
and important appointment and not to be bestowed lightly.
Therefore, it was not unusual for boys and girls of up to
sixteen years of age to still be seen in the $8B_2$. At that age
many of them got their working papers and never did graduate.
Most of the "2"'s graduated and got jobs. Some went on to
trade high schools, and these too were considered low down
in the caste system of the times. A few went on to general
high schools. These last seldom took an "academic course"
which led to college but tried for a "general" or a "commer-
cial" diploma. This too would often elude them because both
the external stigma and the internal one continued to plague
them and to make for serious problems.

I went to eight elementary schools. Each time I went to
another school I was placed either in a "4" class or a "2"
class. Much, I suspect, depended on my own attitude when
I started each new school. If I presented myself fairly well in
appearance with a "nice smile" and so on. I usually went into
the "4" class. If I was sullen, miserable, obviously depressed,
it was the "2" class and instant relegation to second-class
citizenship. There were times when I cared and actually broke
the barriers and went from the "2" to the "4" class and even
once from the "4" to the "3" class. But mostly I became
resigned because any effort was futile and hopeless. After
each classification the school seemed to take pride in being

right and I complied with their "wisdom" and remained where they placed me. Also, there was enormous reluctance to change classification in midyear (transition from the A to B semester) let alone in midsemester. I knew all this without verbalizing it to myself and I never talked of any of it at home and I doubt that my parents had the slightest inkling of this whole caste system. My hopelessness was also promoted by the knowledge that even if I got to a "better class," like Sisyphus with his stone, I would have to start all over again when I came back to still another school in the fall. So I spent my elementary school days mostly in the "2" and "4" classes, and while I am sure I am enriched by the experience because I, too, partook in rebellious action of all kinds and met interesting boys and girls, I also continually suffered from all aspects of the low self-esteem syndrome. Indeed I now feel certain that the whole "2" class experience in large part contributed to an inner sense of hopelessness and futility which were a large part of the substance of the depressions I later suffered from.

I did not suffer too much attrition intellectually because my father introduced me to the public library when I was eight years old and I immediately became a book addict. I suppose in terms of the system my lowest point came in the fifth grade when I gave up hope completely, stopped doing any work in school at all, and was "left back." At home I was busily reading Chekhov, Gogol, de Maupassant, Mark Twain, Jack London, and Darwin, but this did not mitigate the hurt of being left back and the gut feeling that I was somehow a tainted "2" person and would be so forever. Some time after that I was given an extensive battery of tests and came out with the highest IQ in the school. This changed nothing.

At the start of the eight grade the expansive, narcissistic side of me started to emerge and the rebellion had begun. I became competitive. I pushed my way into the various clubs.

Indeed I became the president of the Nature Club, the most prestigious one in the school, and also made a fully conscious and manipulative decision to show how "smart" I was. I went from the "4" class to the "1" class. I could have never done it from the "2" class. I was chosen along with two other boys to try out for Townsend Harris High School, a school for gifted students. A test was involved. I failed since half the exam was on fractions and I must have been en route or out of school and at the beach when fractions were taught. But this did not dilute my newfound esteem, a mixture I would guess now of the real and the synthetic, and I went on to high school with consciousness of second class citizenship fading. I say consciousness and fading because the mind is never wiped clean of anything. The whole hierarchy of a class system—and the connection of the moving from school to school and the "2" class and the cruelty and hopelessness it involved—was almost obliterated and traded for an abhorrence and uneasiness regarding the number "2."

TODAY A PATIENT OF MINE who is now forty-seven years old recalled his first infatuation or "crush" which took place when he was sixteen. She worked in the food section of a small department store in downtown Manhattan, and he went there several times a day to buy something to eat. He recalled that she was about his age or maybe a year or two older—he never did find out, because he never took her out or asked anyone about her. This in no way diluted his obsession with her; on the contrary, this fed it even more because none of the goddess-like attributes he imbued her with were ever diluted by reality. He recalled how he gorged himself on the food he bought from her—fast foods of those days—and got sick several times forcing himself to eat when he wasn't hungry so as to be in her presence. He recalled no sexual feelings or fantasies at all, largely because he had placed her on a plane much too pure and ethereal for these kinds of earthy matters. His feelings of that time were as intense as any he can recall, both painful and enormously joyful and alive. He thought about her day and night and fantasized all kinds of heroic rescue situations between them as well as conversations involving great warmth and friendship. The voice he invented for her—and it was invention because he never heard her speak—was one of delicate beauty. He asked for his waffles (he thinks it was waffles—these kinds of details have escaped memory) and she gave them to him. He paid her and she said nothing, so there was no chance for him to be disillusioned on that score. He says that he can still see her perfectly clearly in his mind's eye and still feels that she was an "exquisitely beautiful" girl. He went on to describe her and included every detail, including her "graceful walk" and the "delicate way" she moved her hands. The crush lasted several months and during that period occupied him completely. He remembers going through the motions of other activities but being in "a kind of haze" and always thinking and fantasizing about her. He did try to muster the courage to speak to her several times but just couldn't do it. I wonder whether his inhibition was due to a lack of courage or to an inner wisdom which kept him from jeopardizing the illusion of perfection.

One day he went to the store and she was gone. He went back periodically for several weeks but she never returned. He is surprised now that while some yearning and disappointment continued for a while, the strength and duration of the pain was not nearly in keeping with the strength of the crush. He continued to think about her but his feelings gradually subsided and then there was a "second crush" on another girl, and the first one was just about over and forgotten. He says "just about," but not quite, because he still pictured her now and then through the years and still does, especially when he is anywhere near where that store used to be. Subsequent infatuations were not the same, not as strong, nor as painful. The second one and those that followed were not at a distance: he got to know each of the girls he became even mildly obsessed with, and of course goddess-like projections gave way to human limitations.

Why is that first crush so powerful? I don't mean the preamble, introductory ones that very small children have; I mean the big and sometimes devastating one of adolescence, the one that goes on smoldering for years and is never really forgotten however long we live. It has little or nothing to do with the boy or girl who is chosen as the object of worship. Certainly a young and innocent imagination makes for proper background music. And there is the advantage of this being a first experience so that one's own inventions are not diluted by any real knowledge. Worship from afar is further aided by lack of reality-complications which usually ensue when contact is made. The most powerful forces at work here are probably anticipation and yearning, both of which have undoubtedly been there from day one. Of course the victim—and we became victims of this obsession which usually occupies our every waking and sleeping hour—is unaware of either anticipation or a yearning for our gods and goddesses. All this goes on unconsciously, subtly, often preverbally and diffusely, never even forming images of any kind but sitting there as an ever increasing force, waiting, waiting not even knowing for what, but waiting for *it* to *happen*. And with this anticipating or waiting there is yearning too, desperately wanting *it* to happen. I think this largely accounts for the restlessness, confusion and general irritability of many adolescents who have not yet objectified or crystallized the anticipation of, or the yearning for, let alone the crush itself but are on the brink of it which makes for very anxious and moody times. *Because* there they are with all this accumulated emotion and super-charged energy and imagery of all kinds waiting to let it all go in one big explosive investment into the fantasy of fantasies—the crush or obsession itself. The emotional investment which takes place is in the crush itself, in the fantasy person, one's projected ideal, and not at all in the real person. This is really an obsession with one's own self-idealization projected to a sexual counterpart who is used as a vehicle sometimes unwittingly. For real emotional investments to take place we need real people, and it is difficult to continue idealizations when people actually get to know each other. So much emotional energy is exploded, let loose into awareness, in that first encounter, never to be quite generated, accumulated, and exploded the same way again. Future infatuations, bordering on and mixed with real relationships, may be deeper and gentler in their way but they seldom leave the highly charged residuals all one's life as does the first crush.

This explosion, the whole process—and I include the awareness, the growing deification, the full force of obsessive preoccupation, in other words the full objectifying of all the disorganized anticipation and yearning that preceded the organization of emotional energy into the crush and the subsequent dilution (or dissipation which sometimes has elements of disillusionment)—can in a way be viewed as one's first "nervous breakdown." I prefer, however, to think of it as one's first break up, big emotional reaction or explosion. Nothing is broken down and these reactions, however painful, always serve some kind of emotional economy as long as we are not destroyed in the process. I think the crush leaves important residuals. It provides continuing elements of romantic reverberations we can draw on for the rest of our lives in a world which is real and sometimes very harsh. At the same time, the dissipation and end of the crush phase and disappointment which follow (in my patient's case it was a mild dissipation but in others this can be very painful) may lead to awareness of reality and provide a significant contribution to adulthood. In other words, this may serve as the beginning of awareness of the difference between illusion and reality, dream relationships and real relationships involving emotional caring about someone else—a real person rather than one's idealized version projected to someone else.

The real danger of a crush is its becoming a chronic process in which the person either goes on from one idealization and disappointment to another or forms a lasting relationship crush intact. This last one leads to a kind of sado-masochistic relating in which one's relating partner is by turns deified and/or vilified over and over again as a fantasy life is projected and then destroyed by reality over and over again. In this case the victim has in fact never moved from adolescence into adulthood and has never recovered from his or her first emotional breakup or emotional reaction.

WHY DO I READ biographies of Hitler? I'm on my fourth, and there isn't much more to it than there was in the first one. I've asked other people the same question and they, too, have come up with no answers which satisfy either me or them. Is it to try to understand Hitler himself, the Hitler in all of us, the era and how it all started? Is it to keep my rage alive and to generate new rage, a kind of substitute for revenge which never took place? Is it a fascination with horror and an acceptable form of masochism? Is it a real interest in history and an attempt to understand more of the machinations of human behavior? Is it vicarious living through identification with victims of the era, tyrants of the era, Hitler himself, satisfying yearnings for power and, yes, even the desire for murder in me?

I suspect all of this is true, that all of it is there, and perhaps this too is part of the fascination, that Hitler helps acquaint us with the "darker aspects" of ourselves—those which we ordinarily make certain are inaccessible. Reading about this monstrous man and monstrous era may be a form of both social (socio-political) and mental hygiene. Of course "never forgetting" is of prime importance in any effort at prevention. It is also important to realize and to continue to be aware of the human capacity for monstrous behavior, which I strongly suspect is not a mutant rarity. But mental hygiene of a more valuable kind takes place whenever we become fully and consciously aware of our "darker sides," of our own monstrous sides, of our greed, death wishes, vindictiveness, sadistic desires, and so on. This is so because bringing these aspects of ourselves up into awareness—even relative awareness—makes dilution of them by our humane, compassionate sides possible. It is when we declare them inhuman (alien to the human condition) and foreign to us, that they become dangerous because they are then repressed. Repression does not mean they go away. On the contrary, while we may lose touch with them and believe they are not there, they are there in darkness, festering and waiting for the possibility of germination and autonomy. No amount of cover-up, neurotic self-idealization makes them go away, nor does warmth, effervescence, love of good food, good music, people, *Gemütlichkeit*. They sit there ready to explode into full-blown existence and in so doing have the capacity to push "compassion" and the sunnier side of human stuff virtually out of existence. This happens, I suspect, whenever and with whomever atrocity takes place, both on the level of individual murders, mass murders, and murders in which whole populations become jailers, executioners, and torturers. There's no making the darker, undesirable aspects of ourselves go away: they are always there. As the man said,

"Nothing human is alien to me," and human means a vast and almost endless panoply of characteristics and possibilities. The darker aspects are most dangerous when we attempt to negate them and to idealize ourselves and when we come to believe that we are "different."

I think the only answer and the only prophylaxis is truth in this as in other situations, and truth in this case means exercising our awareness machinery as regards all aspects of ourselves. To the extent that we bring ourselves into the light of our own vision, without censorship of judgment in terms of good and bad, we make ourselves and the world around us a little safer. The compassion in ourselves does not, I believe, have its chance to develop fully unless it has the opportunity to fully confront the darker aspects of ourselves. Only then can it come to its own full forces as we become fuller human beings. Perhaps on an unconscious level we do this to some extent when we read about Hitler. Of course there are also those who do not read Hitler out of morbid fascination but rather because explosion of their repressed nether sides has already taken place. Their "compassionate" sides no longer exist and they read as a form of worship and full identification, within the constructs of dark paranoid minds in which no humane light shines.

But there's another aspect to reading those books, and this too demonstrates the range of possibility for human grotesquerie. I read with rage, with the desire for revenge, with empathy, pity, and full identification with my fellow Jews and human beings. I read and weep inside for the terrible waste, for the terrible human suffering, inflicted because of utter madness, madness which I have no illusions about, which I know continues today. I read and am enraged by feelings and thoughts regarding all wars and infliction of horror by one human being on another. I weep for the whole nonsense of glory, self-glorification, national glorification, and feel more and more that if we are to survive we must make ourselves aware of our own monstrousness, of our own potential cupidity. I read and I think of my friend Izz Portnoy who says that each country should tear down its self-glorifying monuments and in their place erect monuments depicting their worst atrocities on other people, as reminders of the nether sides of their humanity. And there in the middle of all this, I read Hitler and have a sense of nostalgia for the times in which all this took place. Because, I suppose, I was young in those days, I wore the shining uniform of the U.S. Navy, I was carefree, I had just met Ellie, there was the excitement of war, there was the swing era and the music I grew up with, and it was a time for self-glorification and the possibility of still more glory of all kinds. I knew nothing then of glory being the biggest human killer of them all. So this too I am sure now is why I read about that era, because part of that era, that very era in which so much suffering took place in people I identify with and which makes me rage, also fills me with nostaligc good feelings. Grotesque? Perhaps, but I admit it and accept it because this too and so many other "incongruities" are human after all.

I LOVE THIS CITY of ours—the rich, seething, funky, sweaty, filthy, formal, pretentious, ridiculous, beautiful humanity of it. It is surely a macrocosm of each of us who is a microcosm of it.

Times Square is filthy, seedy, dangerous, sexy, explosive, coarse and vulgar, and is us. This may be heresy but I don't care to change it. Yes, I don't relish muggers and violence, and would that this could be changed, and yet this has been part of the history of all great cities from time immemorial. The smells, the pornography, the crowds upon crowds of people, the schlock shops, the cheap hash joints: we need these, all of these to remind us—more than remind; to put us in touch with—baser aspects of ourselves especially in pretentious times.

And I like pretentious Park Avenue too and the ridiculous doormen uniforms and the blank foolish narrow-eyed pinched faces of those whose parents' parents "made it" for them. And Fifth Avenue and the affectations of those who made *it* on their own, and the panhandlers on Third Avenue, and real people of every and which background on the West Side, and the stores upon stores with all kinds of bargains and Tiffany fancy and elegant goods, and the bridges belching traffic into it all, and Chinatown teeming with life and better food and better bargains than Hong Kong, and restaurant row on Fifty-eighth Street, and columns of glass going up to the sky wherever you look, and the peace and quiet of the great museums and of little Paley Park in the middle of it all, and the grandeur of Lincoln Center and Rockefeller Center and the Forty-second Street library and Grand Central and Penn Stations, and the excitement of coming home—stepping off the train into those enormous welcoming halls, and the bookstores—all kinds, all over, open all hours all days of the week, and the great hotels—the elegant Plaza, the Regency, the St. Regis, and the crass Americana and Hilton and the sleazy ones, and even more sleazy ones where whores make their living, and the million small small stores, and the people who work them, and the whole scene, all of it and much more in a constant state of flux because walk down a street you haven't been on in a while and the whole character of it has changed—new businesses, a new little art center, a new restaurant row, a new ethnic shopping area. And you think you've seen it all and there are always new streets, new buildings, new people, new ideas because this city lives and its energy is in a constate state of movement like only great cities can be.

And there are times I hate it, hate it and myself for being part of it, for not having gone with so many others who left, and I feel that false roots—like economic security, familiarity, and so on—have kept me planted. And planted is what I feel, planted and resigned and hopeless. Because who else would stay in this crowded filthy, dog-feces stinking, poison air carcinogenic ridden, violent, coarse, rotten and rotting place? Who else but those afraid to give up roots which are no roots at all would stay in this ice cold barren uncaring place? Who else would stay in the awful heat in this place where old people die of heat exhaustion, where filthy, starving, uncared-for former mental hospital patients, bruised and battered, lie in gutters and doorways, where bag ladies—old forgotten people—sleep with piles of garbage gathered around them leaning against buildings? One day I see a small wild-eyed looking man walking up and down Third Avenue bumping into woman after woman, hard as he can, trying to knock them down. He doesn't succeed even once, though each of them seems physically jolted and about to fall, they don't seem to notice because this is Bloomingdale's Country and they are preoccupied and anesthetized by visions of shopping orgies they will soon be part of. Today I see and hear a man in the street who walks a few feet and then lets out a blood-curdling scream which lasts a full minute and for a while stops everyone dead in their tracks. But in a matter of minutes they hurry on with their business and pay no attention at all to him. He has already been adapted to and absorbed into the normal pattern of city grotesqueries. In front of Bloomingdale's a young girl screams, "I am Cerebral Palsy" and she does indeed suffer from the disorder and people put money into her hand—lots of money because thanks to "television marathons" they recognize a true representative of a true major illness, and maybe this is the queen of the illness herself. "I am" is so much more effective than "I have."

This hate of mine, what is it all about? What or who am I hating? What is a city after all, a pile of buildings, streets, cars, people? It must be the people and the insane kind of lives we have come to live in this place. Come to live? No, addicted to, because in my hatred I feel I am an addict, otherwise how could I stay on? And I feel degraded by my addiction, my lack of freedom to leave because each time I make even the smallest serious attempt to leave I come running back, fast. So who am I hating at these times? Myself I'm sure, myself and my own chaos, myself, the microcosm of the macrocosm who suddenly suffers attacks in which quiet, gracious, clean living is demanded at once!

These attacks pass in time and leave love for myself, my fellow New Yorkers, my city back in place again. The attack passes very quickly if I see it as a signal to leave for a short while, because leaving inevitably brings back a yearning to go back and going back and coming home always brings on a sweet feeling which obliterates the sourness which preceded.

What is it I'm coming home to? It's more than my home. It's more than the only London or Paris our country has, and there will come a time when this New York will be a source of healthy pride for non-New York Americans (as Paris is for all the French) rather than a symbol of unfamiliar, foreign embarrassment. Then what is it? *It*, this macrocosm of *us*—the microcosms who live here—is the microcosm of the United States of America, and the United States is the noblest experiment mankind has ever undertaken. What other country has attempted an integration of all the diverse people in the world on this scale? Of course this takes time and struggle, and the price is very high. How can an experiment be otherwise—an experience of this magnitude and importance? (Isn't each style of life and way of living together a new experiment for people?) And New York for me represents the kernel of the experiment, the central core and heart of it, and the reminder to the rest of the country that we must never forget our humble origins and noble purpose.

Then why do I hate it? I suspect because I love it. When love is so strong there must be hate too, and perhaps that hate, while it is also surely felt as projections of attacks of self-hate (residuals of which still abide in me), is a reaction to and an attempt to free myself from the bondage of such powerful love. Yes, New York is a place to be young in, and to grow old in, and to feel the stuff of life in at any age or condition. Yes, I've seen non-New Yorkers who say, "New York is a good place to visit but I'd hate to live here," and I've heard others say "I hate New York" and mean it. But mostly their hatred is lukewarm and based on unfamiliarity and an inability to immediately comprehend what must seem like much confusion, paradox, and danger too. But for real hate, hot, deep vitriolic hate, we must look for other sources —like deep, soul-binding, searing, and soldering (because we are soldered to this place) love. And I suppose this hate love is characteristic of life itself and in part defines the vitality of this the most alive, complex, and humanly representative (every kind of culture and person) city in the world.

MY FATHER was the antithesis of the "compliant immigrant."

One day, I must have been in the third or fourth grade, I was pulled out of line, during a fire drill. I was accused of talking. Talking during a fire drill, which consisted of a building evacuation, was practically a capital offense in school terms. You were brought to the assistant principal's office, in this case a Miss Phillips, a truly sadistic martinet who was famous for frightening little children. In those days of teacher deification, a summons to the upper floor administrative offices to face a Miss Phillips was disgrace enough. You remained a marked boy or girl, not only of a "2" class status, but also as a virtual incorrigible. Miss Phillips also was famous for her tirades, each of which lasted at least half an hour. They had nothing at all to do with fire drills and the importance of quick evacuation without distraction. They were sadistic, vindictive, vituperative denunciations often alluding to the "culprit's" weak character, terrible downhill future, faulty bloodlines and downright weak and immoral antecedents, bad manners, undermining the American way, and on and on it went. There was nothing subtle about it except the term "you people," which was used over and over again and which even the smallest New Yorker knew meant either Jew, Italian, or Black. Of course these were days when it was perfectly legal for job and school applications (medical school included) to ask for information regarding religion and ethnic origin, and it was perfectly legal and acceptable to refuse people on this discriminatory basis. Discrimination was not only legal; but it was also proudly practiced from kindergarten right through the whole scheme of things. Miss Phillips was an ardent practitioner of bigotry, and each school usually had a Miss Phillips.

Vilification of the child culprit was not enough: the child was disgraced in another way. He had to bring a parent to school to also suffer Miss Phillips' inquisition and exercise in degradation. Having to bring a parent to school was seen as a disgrace just short of expulsion, and having to witness one's father or mother verbally torn to pieces was more than embarrassing—it was a scene I am sure few innocent children ever forgot. At home most of our fathers were held in the highest and most honorable esteem. Miss Phillips reduced them to cringing, frightened outcasts who were once again being spat on, beaten, and killed by the Czar's Cossacks or their equivalent. Because this is just what happened, and most of the culprits' parents did not speak English well. (Nonimmigrant children were hardly ever guilty of talking on line: teachers and assistant principals never heard them talk because "real Americans" didn't do these things.) The parents understood better than they spoke and Miss Phillips took full advantage of their inarticulateness. She screamed and threatened and told of due consequences and lectured and alluded to Jewish gangsters (Murder, Incorporated), to Italian murderers, to Black rapists, and the like, and never gave these parents a chance to really answer. In the child's eyes his father or mother—and it was usually the father; schools insisted on fathers coming in for the capital offenses even though this meant a day's work lost—was reduced to a groveling, helpless, virtual nonentity. Of course there is little that is more devastating to a child's morale and more traumatic in terms of his own feelings of security and safety.

In my own case, and I felt it was a case and didn't sleep at all in the three days between "being caught" and the day my father appeared, I was particularly overwrought because I was innocent. I hadn't said a word. Maybe I breathed too heavily because I always suffered from chronic sinusitis. This, I think, was my first encounter with injustice, and one of my few personal encounters with false accusation. It has been my only personal encounter with false arrest and being found guilty and receiving sentence without trial. I was punished with a Miss-Phillips-tirade moments after the fire drill, and like all the other childlren regarded bringing my father to school as the worst punishment of all. But all this and to be innocent. It was incomprehensible to me, especially since I knew exactly what I was doing "on line" before I was "pulled out." I was daydreaming. In those days I hated school and I was always involved in one or another kinds of "Walter Mitty" fantasies.

When I gave my father the note summoning him for continuing execution of the imposed sentence, I told him of my innocence, my fears, and my confusions about justice. He spent some time explaining to me that there was no justice,

only man-made attempts to produce justice. He told me of
people who were sent to Siberia because of false accusation
and of a friend of his who was accused and found guilty of
theft (in a marketplace in Russia) and who was permanently
crippled and nearly beaten to death, not because he did anything wrong, but because he was a Jew. He told me about
anti-Semitism, which I had already encountered. He reminded
me that several years after he came to this country (as a great
adventure rather than out of necessity as in the case of my
mother; he was never in any danger of conscription, having
barely survived smallpox and having been a sickly child and
adolescent) how he received news of his father being pulled off
a train and beaten to death during a pogrom. He wept openly
as he told me, a rare thing for my father. He went on and
told me that his father was the kindest and wisest of men
and how people came to seek his counsel and comfort because he was a great scholar and philosopher. He told me
how he arranged for a cousin to go back to Russia and to
bring the rest of his family, a widowed sister and her five
children, to America. He believed in my innocence without
equivocation, and we went on to talk of my boredom and
restlessness in school. I told him nothing of the "2" class
hierarchy. I think now that I felt there was nothing he could
do about it, especially since I never quite articulated the
whole feeling it conveyed in words to myself. But I did feel
that he too would be helpless against the system and also in
the immediate issue helpless against a representative giant of
the system like Miss Phillips. I did not tell him of anti-
Semitic encounters at the beach, of a Mr. Walsh, a middle-
aged neighbor and customer who periodically alluded to my
hooked nose and "how you have to watch you people," and
so on. I didn't for two reasons: I had witnessed my father's
terrible temper and I knew that he was willing to die in any
fight involving anti-Semitism. I had seen him chase people

from his store with a hammer who had made remarks about Jews. I was afraid he might get killed, and I was even more afraid of losing him since I knew how my grandfather died. But even more than that I know now that I was afraid of in any way witnessing his helplessness. This was terrifying because it would immediately negate his omnipotence and shake me to the core in my dependency on him. And my love for him was no small matter—for me to see him hurt or humbled and for him to experience this with me as a witness would be, I was sure, too much for either of us to bear. I think Miss Phillips must have consciously known this about the children and their fathers, but she must have been a very sick woman who could not forego the stimulation and pseudo-alive feelings this kind of interplay brought her. Of course this frightened me more than anything: anticipation of the scene, and my father's helplessness against raging authority, authority gone malignant. My father must have known something of all this because he reassured me again of my innocence, of the fact that talking during a fire drill, while not good, wasn't that bad; that going to see Miss Phillips was not bad at all. I was sure that he was wrong, especially in the last instance, and the few days between our conversation and the visit to the assistant principal were sheer hell for me. I could think of nothing else.

Miss Phillips ranted and raved. She was in rare form, and as soon as she picked up my father's Russian Jewish accent nearly every other phrase alluded to "you people" and "you people come here and then think this and that" and "you people have to learn," and on and on she went while my father listened and I felt terrible and that I had been right after all. She went on and on and he didn't interrupt once, which was very strange for my father, and I should have known that something unusual was about to happen. It did.

She finally ran out of breath and was silent and he lambasted her. I've never met anyone as articulate as my father, particularly when he became vindictive. He called her an "arrogant, bigoted, coarse ignoramus." She turned white but didn't say a word as he went on. He called her a "ridiculous bully and a fool" and said that he would see to it that she would be brought up on charges of "bigotry and incompetence." He said that this time she had picked on the wrong person and would pay dearly for the pain she inflicted on innocent people (I had told him all that I heard from other children). He mentioned almost casually that he would discuss her fully with his friend on the board—"My Jewish friend on the board," he repeated twice. I remember as if it happened this morning because I was being vindicated not only for several days of torture, but also for the "2" class, and for Mr. Walsh, and other incidents as well. He went on and on and she visibly wilted and cringed, and when he stopped she apologized. She, Miss Phillips, apologized to my father in a little girl's voice. The transformation and metamorphosis was complete. He told her to behave and she said she would. The bully had been bullied and cowed. And then he said he wanted a different arrangement for his son. For me at this point being his son meant pure identification with strength. At least for that while second-class citizenship born of the "2" and the "4" class and fed by one's parents having foreign accents (yes, there was self-hate present on that account too) was completely nullified and the sense of exhilaration which lasted for quite a while was unbelievable. I remember it now, and I remember now that sense of a shifting off of a great mass; and this could only have happened if the weight had been there in the first place. I sometimes wonder how many small children go about emotionally depressed without their parent's awareness, who see them as "quiet" or "good" or "bad," or whatever, depending on what form the expression of their depression takes. The arrangement my father wanted was for me to be able to get up and leave the class whenever I felt the need to do that. To my amazement she acquiesced at once. My father said that I read a great deal at home and he wasn't concerned about school work as much as with unhappiness about school, because this would produce a destructive association of study with unhappiness, which could hurt my future. At first I thought she didn't understand, but she did because she suggested that instead of class if I was very restless I could help Miss Brown with the school garden. We left shortly after that, and to my amazement they actually seemed to be on good terms. She, the lord high priestess, executioner of small children and helpless parents, actually fawned all over my father, insisted on shaking hands, and managed to get his reluctant reassurance that for the time being he would not go to his "Jewish friend" on the board of education. I never did find out whether or not he had such a friend. I had a wonderful time in the remaining several months I was at that school, working in the garden and learning much about flowers, trees, seeds, and the like from Miss Brown, who loved gardening and children. This was my first lesson that one can "fight back" even where the enemy is the tyranny of established authority and win. But on the other hand this "example" countermanded my father's explanation of the nonexistence of justice, and my illusion that justice triumphs after all was re-established—for a while.

"FIGHTING BACK" or perhaps just plain lunacy sometimes happens without any plan or preamble at all.

Today is one of my hate New York days. The weather has been bleak for some time now, cloudy, with periodic rain. Air pollution is heavy. The streets look particularly dirty. The buildings are grimy and I've been thinking of other clean, sunny, gracious places. But all this may be pure displacement or at least exaggeration, because what's really been bothering me is quite a bad gum absess. This afternoon I spent an hour —or I should say the dentist spent an hour—operating on the area. For some reason most dentists don't seem to take their own surgery too seriously; few of them premedicate their patients. I've learned that five or ten milligrams of Valium taken an hour before dental surgery is most valuable in relieving strain and in making the whole procedure more palatable both physically and emotionally, but apparently this time the Valium didn't make the procedure palatable enough. The surgery was rather extensive, involving the jaw bone, and the whole right side of my head throbbed when I left his office. I walked along Fifth Avenue in the upper Fifties looking at stores, faces, passing cars, and trying to distract myself to no real avail. For the moment my consciousness was flooded with pain, not a sharp unbearable variety but rather dull and deep yet nevertheless fully permeating. In short I felt miserable and hateful, and was trying to walk off the mood, with little success. Then I had a sense or feeling or sensation that someone was following me. This was at about four o'clock and the street was full of people. I am a native New Yorker and I'm "streetwise," which means being appropriately paranoid. But somebody following me on crowded Fifth Avenue in full or at least smog-semi-full daylight, *me*, six feet three, didn't make sense. I ascribed it to my mood and to my New York paranoia. But the sensation of being followed continued and actually began to provide me with the distraction I was looking for.

And then I knew I was right. I heard the footsteps directly behind me. I walked faster and by this time calculated that I had been followed about three blocks and I could hear the footsteps behind me speed up too. I swerved from one side of the street to another and he swerved too. And then I stopped short. He bumped into me, quickly came around in front of me, and came toward me with one hand out, saying something I couldn't hear. The man was husky, about two or three inches taller than I, in his late twenties or early thirties, and powerful looking. This is as much as I remember of his looks, and I heard nothing of what he said, because I said in pure animal rage, "Fuck off, or I'll kill you." This is interesting because I don't usually use this language and I knew I was angry but not enraged enough to kill, and yet that's how I felt—that if he touched me I would kill him or would be killed in the effort. Also, I have no idea if this was the beginning of a mugging or a request for money; sometimes the line is hazy. Perhaps he only wanted directions, though following me that way for that distance makes this last one unlikely. Anyway, I'll never know because he turned and ran at high speed down Fifth Avenue, nearly knocking over several people as he went. Was this proof of bad intent on his part? I don't know.

Up to the point that this happened I had no idea how I would react—submissive, argumentative, violent, etc.—if confronted in this way. I have heard all kinds of discussions about how to save your life in situations like this but am not convinced any way is better than another since a quick reading of a potential assailant and what he will do if you do this or that is impossible. I am not at all sure I would react this way again. I think much of my reaction had to do with already feeling tormented by my dental onslaught before being confronted by this man, whom I viewed as still another potential tormentor. I am still shocked at the murderous rage that lurks in me and how it can be unleashed and escape conscious control while there I am, supposedly fully awake and in charge of myself. And yet I am not surprised, because I am sure terrible "accident" murders do occur in this way, and I, too, am human after all. But the shock is still there because I suppose I still take some pride, undoubtedly neurotic in some degree, of being "in control." In any case the distraction was complete. I'm still uncomfortable but no longer preoccupied with my jaw, and New York once again seems like the right place after all.

But I must add something that I detect in myself here; it has nothing whatsoever to do with bravery or courage, and yet these are the "hints." I felt good after this happened, very good, too good for just a distraction or for ventilation of rage. I felt good because a kind of macho pride got perked up in me. Yes, for a while I was identified with the same kind of sick prideful infantile male image of glorious bravery that makes us cheerfully go off to war to kill other such afflicted poor souls. Farfetched, taking it too far? I don't think so. Truth is, I could have got killed or saved my life or neither if I listened to him. Maybe he did only want directions, but I felt full of myself, of sick pride in aggression—which must not be confused with healthy "fighting back"—and this is hard, because both can and often are there at the same time.

I'VE HAD KIDNEY STONES on and off for years, and the other day I had to go to the hospital for a checkup and x-rays. I usually have all this done in the doctor's office, and I haven't been a hospital patient (ambulatory, actually, for just a few hours in this case) for years. This is a very large modern institution and nothing like the places I trained and worked in years ago. I had to get out of my clothes, put on hospital pajamas and bathrobe, and wait in a special area until they were ready to take the films. The place was very active, people kept walking in and out of the area, and periodically names were called out over a loudspeaker system.

Waiting there, as a patient, in an unfamiliar place and in unfamiliar clothes I suddenly had a powerful déjà vu feeling. It was really more than that—more than the feeling that all this had happened before. It was as if a whole tableau of feelings had shifted to another time entirely. What must have done it most, I think, is that my defenses were down, I was not in charge, other people were in charge of me. Because suddenly the whole feel and memory of my first day of high school was there again, almost real and palpable, something I had never thought of or had a memory of before, and a whole scene I was not aware had ever registered in me in the first place was there. I suppose the feel of the hospital was much like the school that first day, and my circumstance there brought it on. I didn't feel anxious or disoriented, but I could recall and feel that day in school even better than the day it happened, I suppose because I could at the same time see and feel it from the distance of a great deal of time.

The big public feel of the place, soap smells, pencils, crayons, and paper—white and yellow paper—and ink— black, red, and India thick—and the smell of print, and the smell and look of nail polish—pink, orange, and dark red—and perfume smells and cashmere sweaters—pink and white and light blue—and big breasts and small ones, and words from that time popping into mind: nipples, nubile tits, knockers, pageboy haircuts and crewcuts and long hair and sweaters with varsity letters and ties and shirts and tweed jackets, and teachers; tall, short, young and old, and people and more people and still more people jamming into halls, and the bell ringing and people jamming into halls changing class, room to room, and cafeteria smells, rye bread, french fries, mustard, and the taste of codfish cakes (strange to begin on a Friday but Friday was our first day) and spaghetti and tomato sauce; and voices, low, deep, shrill, whispers, laughs, all kinds, real and phony, forced ones and anxious-trying-to-please ones and lots of giggles and disconnected words and phrases heard here and there—"cute," "fat," "Joan Crawford," "smart," "biology," "must know how to swim to graduate," "Varsity,"

"Glenn Miller," "So what?" "Knock knock"—a janitor in overalls, and back slaps and hugs and punching arms and flashes of faces, wide open laughing, a black face, shy smile, scared one, pinched tight one, rosy cheeks, a blank look, a very sallow sick look, and all the shapes of people possible: wide and narrow, squat, hippy and no hips at all and so many eyeglasses—all kinds—and one bleeding nose and one wheel-chair and a leg in a cast with writing all over it and crutches and the thickest long blond hair and poor clothes and a stunning face: red lips, green eyes, soft skin, white pearls on a soft red sweater and a creamy white neck, and the rooms and more rooms and halls in every direction, and a theater smell auditorium: huge with flags and thick velvety curtains and floor-to-ceiling windows and microscopes—real ones—chalk, desks, blackboards, projectors, slides, pointers and window shutters and Bunsen burners and test tubes and then it all came together as fear in the chest and shakiness in the arms and legs in the civics class. I now vaguely feel this probably had something to do with my not knowing what "civics" was. After our teacher told us it had to do with people and how they lived, especially in cities, I felt better.

They finally took the x-rays and I left the hospital. Now, two days later, that first high school day, some forty years ago, is much more vivid to me than the hospital experience which brought it back to life.

My PATIENT, a man in his early forties, will soon marry a woman slightly younger than himself. He's described her many times and she sounds like a fine and attractive person in all regards. He says that he is in love with her. He goes on to tell me of his considerable infatuation with her, a large part of which involves sexual attraction. We've discussed past in-fatuations he's had, especially those he had when he was very young. He says this time it is different, but then goes on to describe and tell me about this woman in rather idealistic terms. I remind him of disappointments he's told me of in the past and relationships that he's had which broke up precipitously because of disappointments. For some time now we have discussed exorbitant expectations, both in terms of himself and other people, that have stood in the way of having satisfying long-standing relationships. We have talked in the past about how seeking the "ideal mate" is a sure way to keep from marrying. He has come to understand this to some extent and to realize that his not marrying up to now has had little or nothing to do with finding the "right girl" and much more to do with his own inhibition in this area.

But he goes on to tell me that when his current fiancée—and he's had others, many others—wanted to tell him of her past life, including something of her sexual experiences, he refused to listen. He said that he did not want to hear because it "just doesn't interest" him. He knows that "she isn't perfect" and just doesn't care. He told me this in a rather noble, virtuous tone of voice and manner, and I pointed this out to him. At first he refuted any feelings of nobility in this area, but when I reminded him of the double sexual standard he always had as regards men and women, he admitted that I was right. I also said that I wondered if his real motive for not wanting to hear was based on his not wanting his picture of her purity disturbed. He said he knew she wasn't "pure," but, after a good deal of squirming about, admitted that there was truth in this too. While he knew she must have had relationships with other men, hearing about them did, in fact, actualize her not being "ideal." I pointed out that there was nothing particularly virtuous in maintaining false and inhuman—as well as highly prejudiced and sexist—idealizations about one's future mate, or in preventing another person from openly sharing her life's experiences and feelings. He said that he had not thought of this last thing but understood how bottled up and frustrating it could be to be told to withhold information about one's life. I said that I hoped that her desire was to share and not a need to confess, but the need to confess must also be respected. He assured me that she did not have his kind of outlook, felt no guilt about her past, had no need to confess but only wanted to share. I said that I thought this was what I think gut loving, beyond infatuation, was all about: sharing, giving of one's self and feeling free to do just that without fear of moral equivocation, judgment, or reprisal of any kind. He then went on to say that love was a very vague business anyway, and we talked about this for a while.

Is love vague or impossible to describe or put into words? I suppose part of it is, the chemistry part, the infatuation. In a way it is like trying to get someone to feel the taste of chop suey by describing and analyzing the ingredients. It doesn't work. One must taste the chop suey.

But there is another part, perhaps the most important part, the part that has the potential for growing, evolving, and lasting. This part in no way precludes or dilutes the chemistry if that sexual chemistry is fairly healthy. If the chemistry is of a sado-masochistic variety, a "Who's Afraid of Virginia Woolf" kind of thing, this part will hardly exist, and if it comes into existence at all it will probably nullify the sexual part. But if the sexual relationship has deeper roots and derives at least some excitement from a healthy warm desire to receive and to give and to be close to, then this part will both enhance and transcend the chemical faction. By "transcend" I mean it will be there and have its own importance over, above, and beyond the realm of sexuality, even though sexuality will be enhancing to this aspect of relating also. The faction I speak of here is *friendship, real friendship,* which I believe may well be the most important aspect of love. And *real friendship* is not precluded in sexual relationships. On the contrary, a sexual relationship without it is not a loving one. I do not preach any kind of morality here about sex. I recognize and respect sexual relating devoid of friendship. I also respect sex with hardly any relating at all, because sex can take place on an almost purely mechanical level. But I do not believe this is love. I do not believe that infatuation with or idealization of another person is love either. These may or may not be there but they are not evidence of love. For me love always involves friendship, and friendship involves openness, tenderness, and intimacy. Big love involves much openness, much tenderness, and much intimacy.

To be open is no small matter and is not the result of an act of will but rather comes of much practice. Initially, a great deal of struggle may be involved too, because without awareness many of us are used to relating on a closed basis, revealing as little to ourselves and about ourselves as possible —especially as regards our feelings. Openness cannot take place with others if we are not open with ourselves. If we do not know how we feel, how can we tell others how we feel, and how can we appreciate other people's feelings when they reveal them to us? We must be open to our own feelings, moods, thoughts, sensations, and ideas if we are to be open to those of other people, and openness is the first and crucial dynamic in that all-important friendship part of love.

I suppose tenderness involves treating that which is received both from ourselves and from others with great care and non-judgmental respect and compassion, and with full awareness that "nothing human is alien" to anybody. Tenderness stands against harsh judgment, competition, vindictive triumph, and the whole right/wrong equation. Where tenderness is practiced, people are less interested in who is right and who is wrong, and more interested in understanding each other and helping each other to better understand one's self. I view the practice of tenderness as an ongoing analysis between people because in analysis the goal is always an extension of insight rather than moral equivocation and judgment or punishment. Tenderness makes for increased openness, and where tenderness is lacking closure takes place.

Intimacy cannot take place without openness and tenderness, and of course there are people who have lived together for many years and who are not at all intimate. Intimacy involves mutuality and sharing, and goes beyond openness or receiving information about one another's feeling. Intimacy also involves empathy, sympathy, and striking resonant chords in each other in response to one another's feelings. For this mutuality (intimacy) to take place a process of common interests, involvements, and emotional investments must be initiated and sustained. Intimate people share common interests and share common loved ones. Very intimate people build a common frame of reference and their own intimate language, the language of their love. Various symbols and subtle nuances, often non-verbal, are shared by them in mutual understanding of life situations they find themselves in. Intimate people are keenly attuned to each others' feelings, moods, needs, proclivities, desires, frustrations, yearnings, pain. In short, they are intensely alive and receptive to each other's existence.

These, then—openness, tenderness, and intimacy—for me comprise the principal factions of love and these are not ethereal entities. One day I intend to explore their dynamics and interrelationships in detail. I believe that observation of love on the basis of openness, tenderness, and intimacy tells us much about any relationship, and that includes the prognosis of a relationship's progress. However much love is declared by people involved, lack of any of the three basic factors is bound to make for difficulty, or a non-loving relationship, or one devoid of real friendship. Where the factions are present and alive and well, we are in fact dealing with genuine friendship, the very important substance of love regardless of whether or not the word love is mentioned.

ELLIE CALLED MY MOTHER this morning and my mother complained that I don't call her often enough. From her point of view she is absolutely right: I don't call her often enough to provide the attention and respect she wants or feels she needs from me. Unfortunately, calling her is not easy for me and not something I casually avoid because "I just don't feel like it" or because "It's annoying." I don't call because for the last few years it has been depleting and depressing. The conversation never varies and is actually no conversation at all but rather a monologue of complaints (mainly physical) by her. This time Ellie said, "Well, let's face it, Ted is neglectful of you" (true in her terms) "and is a bad son; he's just no good." When they hung up Ellie told me that my mother seemed satisfied. However she called back a few hours later and told Ellie that she should not say "things like that" about me, that "Ted is good." I understand her dilemma. On the one hand she is angry with me and feels that I am "no good." But on the other hand this spoils her idealization of me from which she still derives a shred of personal prestige, and disturbs her image of herself as a "good mother." How can a "good mother" have a "bad son"?

Why is it depleting for me to call her? In office practice I hear people complain, distort, berate, project, and make unfounded claims for hours on end and this doesn't deplete me. Yes, *she* is my mother, but this is not an answer. Manipulation by her, even at this late date, and evocation of guilt are not answers either, because her manipulations are essentially ineffectual, and my response to her self-imposed martyrdom is minimal and I do not feel guilty. I think my feeling of depletion comes rather from the very business of lack of dialogue or conversation between us and the gut knowledge that I have no impact on her. There is no give and take between us: she really does not hear what I say. I become a sounding board—and not even that, because she does not respond to reverberations from me. My own narcissism, both healthy and sick, prevents me from playing out the role of the nonentity listener. I want to be heard, however little and however rarely. In this regard my frustration is total and this frustration of my own expectations is both depleting and depressing. I have struggled with these expectations and have attempted to reduce them to zero, to be satisfied with putting in a call, listening, saying yes a few times, and nothing else, but it doesn't work. I think my respect for her and for us and our relationship, full of give and take, that we had for years is still there and makes this kind of "act" impossible.

Some time ago my mother indicated that she does not get ample respect and that in fact, eighty-year-old people are not respected and treated with ample dignity in our society. She is right, unfortunately, about the shabby treatment of the aged; this to me represents the epitome of a self-hating society. But I pointed out that a reclusive life style does not generate real dignity, respect, or the social intercourse necessary for this kind of respecting to take place. I pointed out, gently, that she chose to remove herself from life's activities and from people generally, including friends and relatives. For a moment I thought we might get into a real exchange. She answered that I expect too much of eighty-plus-year-old people. I said that she was in no way infirm, but even if she felt she was, people were willing to come to her but she always turned them (with the exception of her children) away. She repeated that my expectations of her were disproportionate to her age and condition, and went on to complain of lack of respect. And she is right, because it is difficult to respect someone regardless of age who evidences neither self-respect or human involvement on anything resembling a substantial level. I tried to have her explain what she meant by "respect," but she was only interested in repeating the complaint rather than sharing in any kind of elucidation that might lead to real change. Of course "real change" between us must involve give and take, and this involves more than a "sounding off exercise," but this remains all she wants for now and I am at best a reluctant, inconsistent, and infrequent participant.

IT WAS A GOOD DINNER PARTY. There were only eight people, no posturing or pretense, and very little small talk.

Eventually the conversation got around to various activities geared to self-satisfaction, and the one we came to concentrate on was "helping other people." We made it clear that we all meant "real help" as differentiated from any kind of exploitative, self-serving manipulation or pseudo-help designed to supply narcissistic baggage to either helper or helpee, however benevolent it would seem. Therefore, we eliminated any kind of activity whose prime purpose would be to elevate the helper to self-glorifying feelings of altruism. We pretty much agreed that helping another or others, without either healthy or neurotic motivation to help ourselves in the act—no personal side benefit at all—gives enormous and maybe even ultimate personal satisfaction. In that regard, helping others does become the most selfish thing we can do.

Selfish is a poor word to use in this connection; we might better use the phrase "healthy self-satisfaction" in its place. But regardless of what we call it, and however "corny" or simplistic it may seem, helping others is one of the great if not the greatest form of delivering satisfaction and help to one's self. We can even say that it is therapeutic and curative. Therapists, even though they get paid, inevitably have the experience of feeling better as a direct result of helping another person to feel better. This feeling better and even exhilaration in helping others is the result of something deeper than the power involved or the satisfaction of professional pride and a job well done. It seemed to me that there are essentially two dynamics at work, though they are really part and parcel of each other: one is the exhilaration experienced when we become aware of, and feel, the curative power of being human. I am not speaking here of exclusive experiences in medicine or therapy but rather help given in all human encounters. All human beings have this power or curative ability, and I hasten to add now that I speak of nothing mystical, no faith healing, no miracle cures for dread illnesses. We all have curative ability which is derived from our humanity and can serve us through serving others and occurs in the process of relating. Yes, as I said before, in helping others we help ourselves, and in this regard—through human involvement and caring and I suppose the kind of open, tender, intimate friendship love I spoke of earlier—we have considerable power to help or cure, if you will, others and thus ourselves. The response of people to real caring and sharing when the genuine article (no act will do) is presented, is enormous. When someone else cares, shares, and in effect invests himself, his feelings, this mobilizes assets and self-curative resources on the part of the person being helped which too often he cannot tap on his own.

Now for the second part, which is really a continuation of and inseparable from the first: *how does this help the helper?* In helping other people (and this includes all kinds of help but applies especially to help which taxes the helper and makes him work in order to use his own resources) the helper taps, brings to life, mobilizes, and integrates his own resources and assets. This makes those resources available for the helper's own use but it does more than that. It also makes him aware of his resources and strengths and real power or potency, and identifies him with these strengths which become reawakened each time he activates them by helping others. This activity immediately increases self-esteem and if repeated often enough as a form of exercise can contribute significantly to a permanent increase in self-esteem.

This means that we need to do for others in order to do for ourselves, just as we need to do for ourselves in order to do for others, because without sufficient nourishment of self there isn't sufficient self to do for others. All this is in keeping with the human need to relate to other human beings and in part accounts for the kind of inner shrinkage and emotional blunting and even death which characterize seclusiveness. This may in part explain the kind of frustration and depletion I feel in regard to my mother. When needed help is not available the effect is destructive, but when the need to give help is thwarted the effect may be even more destructive. In a larger sense, her closure to my giving prevents me from receiving my own best therapy. I told our discussion group at dinner about this and I also said that in this regard, blessed is the person who receives openly and graciously. Accepting help which is needed is no small matter; it often involves a put down of sick pride, a put down of competition and the notion of being low man in a mythical hierarchy, and it takes a big dose of healthy humility. To complete the give-and-take cycle, the gracious receiver is also the helper, because in his open acceptance of help he helps the helper. One of the men in the group asked if I tried to get my mother to help others. She is very bright, intact, and has considerable resources, and I've told her this many times and have tried to get her to help other people. But she refuses to even entertain the possibility. For the moment (and I always believe change is possible) she is preoccupied with herself and, as is always the case in this kind of sick narcissistic self-involvement, she believes that she has nothing to give to anyone else and not enough substance to receive anything anyone else gives to her, thus completing a very vicious and resistant cycle.

After Ellie and I left that evening, we talked about all this for a while and she asked if help, any kind, but especially the kind that represents real caring and involvement of self is actually the substance of *love*. I think that we have to be careful about *love* because the term has come to mean an idealized state from which much misunderstanding, disappointment, and misery ensue. I have heard so many sick and distorted claims made by people on the basis of "love" which to me is "anti-love": "If you love me you would know what I'm thinking." "If you loved me you would have done this or that." "If you loved me you would give up this or that interest." The term "love" as promoted by our culture is much distorted and confused, and involves exorbitant inhuman expectation. This is the antithesis of "love." But if we view giving or helping others as openness, tenderness, and intimacy in action, and see this process as love, then I am in agreement. Helping others may then be viewed as the essence, or at least an essence, of friendship and therefore as love—love which is based on and integrates openness, tenderness, and intimacy. Giving of self may then be viewed as representation of this kind of "reality love" which is based on and integrates openness, tenderness, and intimacy. The practice of openness with others enhances openness with our own feelings and makes for greater integration of our feelings and cohesivness of self. Practicing tenderness with others enhances compassion for self and greater acceptance of all that is human about us. Intimacy with others increases self-exploration and greater self-knowledge, diminishing our fear of any aspects of ourselves that we tend to repress because they may be out of keeping with society's standards. This also minimizes the anxiety which accompanies potential emergence of these aspects of ourselves into consciousness, because in the process we learn to welcome and to accept emergence of all aspects of self. Giving of self may then be viewed as representative of this kind of "reality love" as differentiated from idealized notions of love. I am convinced that there is little, if anything, in human experience which is as therapeutic and nourishing to our soul and substance as this love.

I GOT INTO A CAB near the Port Authority Bus Terminal yesterday evening. The taxi driver was a professorial sixty-year-old man who told me he had been driving a cab for more than thirty years. I say "professorial" because the man obviously loved to expound on various subjects and he was quite articulate in his renditions. He told me that he liked driving because he met all kinds of people, saw all the city sights—and there was much to see—and because driving a cab took care of both his laziness and restlessness. He could sit while he moved. He owned his own cab and therefore felt like both the president and janitor of a company, as well as all the employees in between—a small company, but one which made him an independent entrepreneur who could work any hours he chose. He gave me a lecture on "seedy people" who hang around all kinds of city terminals and ports of entry, railway stations, bus terminals, ship ports, airfields, and "any kind of bazaar that is going on." "Where else would petty thieves, con men, pimps, whores, pickpockets, muggers, and beggars find the goods they need and so many potential victims gathered? These crowds let them get lost fast in the masses of people. It's relatively safe, and most of all they like to be near exits so they can make easy and quick getaways if necessary. Just get on a train or bus and leave the city." He told me that throughout history borderline criminal people were attracted to these places. I did not ask him what research he had done to get this information, but he was probably right. He went on to say that "they" in large part accounted for the seedy appearance of what could otherwise look like the magnificent places they really were, because "they" themselves are seedy looking and "they soil and litter wherever they live, and they live in these terminals even though they are all migrant bums and call no place home." I listened like a good student and didn't offer any counter opinion because I got the feeling that he had thought this out carefully and was not open to any thought which might disturb his thesis.

The word "terminal" intrigued me. I thought back to the various carnival people I knew at the beach when I was young. Most were so full of hope and optimism, however down and out they seemed. Hope, that each new summer season would be better, would do "it" for them ("it" represented different things for each of them—to own a house, to live in a warm climate, to drive a Cadillac). I thought of the people who hang around the cities' various station waiting rooms and wondered what they are really waiting for. For any of them arriving at any of the cities' "terminals," these for the moment marked the termination of a trip, but I bet that for most of them these "terminals" represented the possibility and hope of a "beginning" rather than an "ending," even if that hope was for success in making some shady "score."

But for these "outsiders" don't these places also represent gathering points where they can stay and feel less lonely? Because these people, for whatever reasons, are not part of the mainstream of society but are still capable of loneliness. It is possible that a great train station like Penn Station can provide people needed to make others feel less lonely and at the same time ensure sufficient anonymity so that there is no threat of too much closeness. I remember seeing in consultation a young man who came from a rather middle-class conventional background and who was suffering from severe acute anxiety. For the moment he could not tolerate closeness to people. Conversation and the concentration it took were too much for him to endure. But at the same time he was lonely and also afraid to be alone. He told me that he discovered that he felt better walking around Kennedy Airport. The hustle and bustle of people coming and going made him feel better, while at the same time no social give-and-take were demanded of him.

Vagabonds, I think, feel comfortable at points of departure because these places represent their way of life, that is, their particular adaptation or lifestyle. They do not live in the "middle of cities" either geographically or in terms of ordinary "people activities" or "people involvements." They live on "the edge," on the perimeter, in a touch-and-go kind of life which is devoid of commitment and involvement with ordinary "people activities." Yet even they need people, if for no other reasons but to mitigate loneliness and to feel free of involvement from people. This sounds paradoxical but really isn't: they need people to remind them of their freedom from involvements with people. But they also need the constant possibility and, more than that, the promise of free access to other places. Having myself been oriented to moving constantly from one home to another as a child, Ellie and I still moved a great deal in the last thirty years. She hardly moved at all as a child and only went to one elementary school and one high school. Yet she adjusted quickly and easily to each new house while my adjustment was poor. I realize that for her, arrival at a new place meant "settling down," and she was used to that. For me it meant no moving, for at least a while, and moving was the thing I was most used to. I realize now that I've been most comfortable once the decision to move has been made, and this is the very time she feels uncomfortable and in a state of upheaval. Perhaps the vagabonds have solved this problem by living in or close to points of arrival and departure.

But the taxi driver was angry at these people, and each time I've moved I've incurred all kinds of thinly veiled hostility from people I know, too. Is there any kind of connection? I think there is. I suspect most people would like to move more. They would like to be free of inner constrictions and would like to break through all kinds of inhibitions and paralyzing inertia. They would like to escape conventional traps comprising the need to compete, succeed, to win, to get more and more and still more. They would like to be free to be fly killers again or for the first time, that is, to regain or for the first time to experience thoughtless spontaneity. I suspect that for the taxi driver, on an unconscious level, the people who live on fringes represent this kind of freedom. He hates them because they are not locked into taxis and do not have to be presidents of any companies at all. They don't have to rationalize that they can work any hours they choose because they don't seem to have to work at all. Of course this is not true: most of these people are as compulsive about their "lifestyle" as the taxi driver may be with his, most of them are hurt and frightened people and have much in common with so many conventional people who are also terrified of commitment and involvement. The vagabonds act out their fear of "entrapment" and live as vagabonds. The others ostensibly enter into society's activities and relationships but hold back feelings and seldom do completely capitulate to free and full involvement with other people. On the surface, people who feel ensnared by their own rules and society's conventions despise the "bums and tramps" and people who live on "the fringe." But on a deeper level they envy and admire them for the illusion of uncaring freedom with which they are imbued. As to my "friends" and the hostile jibes they make each time I move, I've noticed that most of it comes from people who never move either geographically or in any other way. People I know who are engaged creatively never seem to be moved by my moves one way or another.

THIS MORNING I got a letter from a doctor I know who asked if I can refer patients to him. I can't. He is well-trained. He is dedicated to his work. He is very bright, and maybe talented too, but I feel that he doesn't like people. He's interested in their problems and interested in resolving them. Pathology and the dynamics involved interest him, but I know this man, he was a student of mine and I consistently had the impression that he doesn't really care for people.

I believe that it is of paramount importance that a therapist likes and even more than that, loves a patient. Of course I do not mean the "in love with" infatuation kind of component. The love I speak of here is of the all-important OTI (openness, tenderness, intimacy) kind. Too many therapists, in their fear of countertransference, and in their confusion as regards OTI and infatuation, maintain so much aloofness and distance that forthcoming human help becomes impossible. Without giving of self "therapy" becomes a highly intellectualized process and has very limited value. People given to depression—and this includes the majority of us— need love to stimulate love in themselves. Many doctors love confrontation with pathology, the challenge of diagnosis, and the victory of amelioration (cure is too rare to even be seriously considered) but this is not enough. The real "therapeutic touch," the one that touches the soul, the stuff of our deepest humanity from whence springs our own constructive forces, comes from loving people, loving the human condition.

A friend of mine on the faculty of a large and well-known medical school interviews potential candidates for admission. The questions he and other interviewers ask involve grades, academic interests, general interests, achievements, and so on, but do not include the vital questions "Do you love people?" or "How do you feel about people?" or "Are you capable of loving people?" Does the interviewer ask himself this key question regarding the applicant? If he does, where in the hierarchy of important considerations in choosing future doctors does love of people appear? Of course even if the interviewer does not formally ask the question of the candidate, or even of himself regarding the candidate, much along these lines must surely be taking place on an unconscious level. The interviewer comes away with an "impression" based on the candidates "warmth," "vitality," "humor," "sophistication about people," and the like. The interviewer also knows whether or not he likes the candidate and perhaps he also knows or feels, though not in so many words, that the candidate conveys an impression which makes potential love of the candidate possible. These are the most valuable prognostic signs in evaluating the candidate's capacity for loving people, for people who are "loving" are themselves "lovable." Of course one interview may not convey this information. Several and even many may be necessary, and the information will not be forthcoming or received at all if the interviewer himself or herself is not a loving person. But even if the interviewer puts great store in the candidate's ability or lack of ability to love people, how much of a role does this play when the admissions committee makes its final choice? I'm afraid very little, and I'm sure this is reflected in the medical population. When the criteria for admission are primarily based on grades, competition, and hierarchical standards of accomplishment we may expect technical expertise and competence, but is this enough?

The people to whom I refer people must be people who love people. They must be competently trained too. One criterion does not preclude the other. But when I refer a patient I try to make a proper "match." This means that the patient must be referred to a therapist who is capable of loving that patient. Yes, there are patients whom very few people can love, but for them it is even more important to find the "right" doctor because these are usually the most battered, hurt, and vulnerable people. For these people, brilliant interpretations are not enough and verbal acceptance is not enough. For the vastly damaged among us only real caring helps, and the difference between the real and synthetic stuff can be perceived at once.

I COMMITTED MYSELF to handball when I was ten years old, reached my peak at sixteen, and quit when I was twenty-three. I was not consciously aware of why I "chose" handball until years after I stopped playing. We seldom ever became aware of unconsciously determined motivations. But the unconscious goes along undisturbed by interference of conscious machinations and dictates its desires, both sane and insane, and without benefit of psychoanalysis we usually comply.

Why any sport at all for me, and why handball? Because then as now the culture demanded that male pride could only be assuaged by some kind of physical, competitive skill. To accept myself and to be accepted, however superficially, by contemporaries or even adults in each new place I found myself in, or at least to not be regarded as peculiar (or even worse, "queer"), demanded some kind of involvement with "sports."

Handball was perfect in several ways that my unconscious undoubtedly "perceived" without my sitting down and figuring it out at all. It required no money. Single wall handball required just that: a wall, some pavement in front of it, and a small hard black ball, cheap in those days. There were "courts" in every neighborhood I ever lived in and there were actually regulation courts eventually put up by the community at the beach. Looking back now I realize that I barely heard of tennis in those days. It must have been a game for wealthy people; I don't remember seeing a tennis court in any neighborhood I lived in. Handball also had the great advantage of requiring very few people to play. There are only four players in "doubles" and two in "singles," and if necessary you can play alone since it requires no adversary just to hit the ball against the wall. This not requiring many players as do team sports had more than one advantage. We would arrive at the beach in late April or the beginning of May and leave sometime in October. There were very few people, and even fewer my age, who were there for several months, except for July and August when the "real summer people" were there. In this regard I had a great advantage over the "real summer kids" (people who came for vacations rather than business) because I practiced handball in April, May, June, September, and October while they were involved at home in team sports. The other all-important thing about handball not being a team sport was that you didn't have to be chosen by a team in order to play. This was very important to me since I was perpetually the new kid on the block, and this saved me from having to prove myself repeatedly. There was something else too. On a team you have to answer to your teammates. In handball you had only yourself or at most a partner to whom you were accountable. I never figured any of this out in those days, but I am sure that defensive maneuvers are never consciously figured out but nevertheless stem from need and unconscious logic. I "loved" handball. I could love it with ease and could approach it with the most relaxed attitude precisely because it satisfied various needs without producing any special anxiety of its own. But in looking back I came to realize there was something else too. I became very good at the game, and this was not because of speed, coordination, or brilliance in strategy. I played four and five hours a day for years, and of course some skills inevitably developed, but this did not account for my winning either. Mostly I won because I hit the ball so hard. I hit it hard almost all the time—many times when hitting it easy would have been better strategy. Why? Because all the resentment I felt—and there was much of it, especially the rage I felt at always being a "2" class person, new on the block, and an outsider—went into hitting that little black ball. In handball there is a term, "killer." Hitting a "killer" or "killing" the ball meant hitting a perfect shot, one so low along the ground or so strong and fast that it could not be returned by one's opponent. I "killed" the ball many times and this was largely the way I won games. But my killers were based more on speed of the ball than on position. Did handball and killing the ball and the aggression I expressed that way save me from other disastrous consequences? I don't think so. I think it was relieving, but I think it also delayed the inevitable. There was still a great deal of anger I repressed or better yet depressed, still a good deal of striving for impossible, self-idealizing glorification, and the consequent disappointments and falls from these positions which eventually resulted in painful anxiety and depression. No amount of handball or other sublimation could get at the core of the problem; of course psychoanalytic treatment was necessary to give me the insights I needed to cope on a somewhat better level. Did handball give me self-esteem? I don't think so. I doubt that competitive involvement ever does. It gave me surges of excitement, self-importance, and satisfaction of vindictive triumph characteristic of sadistic victory over one's opponent, in my case representing displacement from anger at a difficult life situation. But this is not self-esteem and does not build feelings of real security. It is synthetic stuff, and even in the middle of a synthetic surge of self-confidence I think the feelings of self-doubt and fear of

not being able to sustain an exalted status (based on someone else's loss, which is a clear reminder of one's own potential
to lose) are always there. I still very much feel that real self-
esteem must be based on real compassion for self which
eventually leads to compassion for others. This, the real thing,
has no strings attached, no conditions, no ifs or buts, just
acceptance of all human characteristics regardless of how
society views them. In self-esteem based on this stuff, winning
does not play any role at all.

Several things happened during my sixteenth summer. As
I said earlier, I reached my peak in handball. I beat the four
wall national champ in a single wall game. Let me say that
(1) he was on the decline at this point in his handball career,
(2) he was the four wall champ, a game that is different from
single wall and which I didn't play until I went to college,
(3) he was tired, having played several games before he
played me, and (4) he underestimated me since he never saw
me before, and of course knew nothing of my need to kill
the ball (which I didn't know about either). But these factors
did not in any way alter the glory that was mine on that day
or in hundreds of days which followed. I beat an official handball champion and several of my friends saw me do it, and
an instant myth of my handball prowess was created and
sustained for some years. Years later when I went into the
navy I still tapped that experience and it made me feel that
I had a secret weapon should I encounter unpleasant experiences in this still another new encounter.

Four wall handball did come in very handy because when
I first entered the navy I played in tournaments and was
accorded all kinds of special privileges. The navy was very
good to athletes who could in any way enhance the glory of
the "base," "the company," or the navy itself. This was the
first time I had encountered "special treatment" of any kind
(we did not have to make any kind of formations, were served

much better food, were treated almost as equals by superiors) and I was quite surprised that this occurred on the basis of handball. Having come from generations of Talmudists I am sure that I was convinced that if any special privilege existed in life it would come as a result of scholarly struggle and surely not *handball*. When I was twenty-three and well out of the navy I was introduced to the then New York State four wall handball champion. In four wall handball there are players and players, meaning that it is almost as if there are invisible lines separating different classes of players. If a player of a superior class plays one of an inferior class the game often winds up with dramatic differences in scores, because in this game the really skilled player can make it almost impossible for the player of lesser skill to even return the ball. In four wall handball I had even less skill than in single wall but by this time had developed much greater strength and an extremely strong shot. This "strong shot" saw me through many wins in the navy and gave me the illusion of skill, too, because the players I encountered were of an inferior class to me and could hardly return the "fast ball" I hit. But it was another matter entirely with the state champion. My strong ball was of no consequence to him. He hardly moved, and didn't need to in order to return my ball. He simply waited until it ricocheted off the walls and then placed it exactly where he wanted to, out of my reach. He had complete control of the court, the ball, and me. He was in a higher handball category, light years above mine. We "played"—actually he toyed with me—and I never worked so hard, three games and I hardly scored at all. After that day, I never played again. By this time I did have a chipped shoulder bone, from years of playing a "strength" no-skill game, and it did hurt when I played, and this was the reason I gave myself for stopping, but of course this wasn't the reason at all. I stopped because if I could not maintain the illusion of being the best or of someday becoming the best, I wouldn't play. *Being the best* had infinitely more to do with vindictive triumph and self-glorification than it had to do with the joy of playing. At the time of "my defeat" I felt no great sorrow and was not conscious of "making up my mind" or "deciding" not to play anymore. My unconscious took care of that: it made sure that I would suffer no other blows to synthetic self-esteem or neurotic pride because I went on to other things, accepted my chipped shoulder bone status (the wounded hero image helped too), and "somehow" never played handball again.

I MET A GIRL that summer. Her name was Lee and she was sixteen years old too. Sixteen is a particularly difficult age for boys vis-à-vis girls: girls much younger are usually too young to be interesting, and girls of sixteen usually consider boys their age as "kids" (they are probably right). But I had no trouble meeting her and we hit it off right from the start, so much so that we quickly became friends, good enough friends so that no crush developed either way. Crushes are best developed at a distance, and we talked a lot, got to know each other real well, so there was very little distance. But I liked her very much and was quite attracted to her. She was a beautiful dark girl with black flashing eyes and great vitality and exuberance. I wonder if I would have met her at all if I hadn't beat the national champ. The immediate self-confidence (however synthetic) this brought, I think, made it possible for me to start a conversation with her. As it turned out I spent a great deal of that summer with her and her family (they were at the beach for the season) and got to know her mother and older brother quite well.

Lee had no affectations at all and, as it turned out, was no less or more mature or sophisticated than I was. I think we held hands and I think we hugged. I don't think we ever kissed. Why not? I don't know, because I know we were attracted to each other. But those were strange times and handball confidence took me no great distance. Lee had an older sister who was married to a senior medical student and they lived in Arkansas where he went to school. Her mother confided in me that she would be much happier if her older daughter were married to a businessman. In fact, she said that she secretly—and not so secretly—hoped that her son-in-law would quit school or even flunk out, because she would be very happy to take him into the family business. I recall that they were in some phase of the milk business and were very wealthy people by standards of those times. I cannot describe the shock I felt when I realized that Lee's mother meant what she said. I had wanted to be a doctor since I was four years old, and I just couldn't imagine that anyone in this world would not want to be a doctor, or would possibly prefer that a relative who could be a doctor, would be or do something else, let alone become involved in business. I knew the importance of money: we worked very hard for it, but I had no concept of either power or prestige to be gained through money, let alone anything about deeper or sustained gratification or even excitement that making money could bring. Lee's mother tried to explain all this to me as best she could, and though I understood her intellectually, I had no gut feeling about it. I still felt, and I suppose I still do, that medicine was *IT*, and there just could not be anything else to compare to *IT*. The strange thing is that I distinctly remember that Lee agreed with me and not with her mother, but this did not at all seem to perturb her mother, whose attitude continued to convey the message that in marrying a future doctor her older daughter had somehow married beneath herself. To my amazement, from what she said she equated doctors with all kinds of people whose "services can be bought." She was not crass or coarse about this, but simply honest in how she felt. I was astounded! But this was a valuable exercise in diluting my egocentricity. It was also educational because this was my first confrontation with the fact that people could and often do have value systems and frames of reference utterly different from my own.

I learned another "lesson" as well. In the middle of the winter following that summer I called Lee in the city and found out that she had married a rich businessman ten years older than we were. I learned that girls do listen to their mothers even when they seem to disagree with them.

That too was the summer that Harold Waite came home from medical school. Harold's father ran a small bathhouse —showers and lockers—near the beach where we had killed many flies during that summer a few years earlier. Harold knew about my obsession with medicine from conversations we had held several summers earlier. At that time (I must have been about twelve) he gave me several lectures on anatomy and let me keep his Gray's *Anatomy* overnight several times. I was fascinated, but more than that I felt accepted and felt that I belonged. At no time did I have the smallest doubt that I would go on to medical school, the "2" class be damned. I must say that while my father never sold me on the idea or pressured me in any way in this direction, he was completely supportive of my goal. However bad my grades were or poor my school adjustment was—and at times they were very bad—he always believed, and he said as much many times, that I would be a doctor. Even when I got left back in the fifth grade, his ultimate confidence in me was not shaken, even though some cousins and aunts felt disgraced. Looking back now I realize I had to get left back: my sister, six years older than I, had skipped six times. What else could I do for attention? I'm sure, too, that this was largely a function of at least some emotional disturbance, most of it undoubtedly due to considerable depressed rage and a need to express it somehow. But my father said that grades and early schooling didn't matter because I had "the motivation and the ability and it would come through." I believed him, and so did Harold Waite, because that summer of his graduation he gave me a Merk manual. That book became my bible that year. It was the most fascinating book I had ever encountered. I read and reread it several times, unwittingly memorizing symptoms, pathological physiology, syndromes, and treatment for every and which condition. Years later all of it was very familiar to me when I encountered it again in medical school. I think one of the things that got me about the manual was its extraordinary compactness. Holding it, I used to have the illusion that I had the whole of medicine in my hand. Of course it was no small matter that Harold Waite gave it to me. To me he was a friend—a respected friend who respected me—and no small hero, Lee's mother notwithstanding.

My patient, a young woman who has a two-year-old little girl, felt awful. She had been crying all night.

She told me that her daughter, a particularly beautiful, bright, and lively child, ran out of the house yesterday morning and cavorted on the lawn in the middle of the heavy rain. It had been cold and raining for more than a week. She understood that the child felt cooped up and bored and finally gave way to her natural exuberance and ran out to play in the rain, but my patient, seeing her out there "happy in the rain" but getting "all wet and cold," ran out, grabbed her, "spanked her hard, and yanked her inside." The daughter cried and was miserable for a few hours. My patient cried and has been miserable since. In associating to the incident she said that she felt a sense of heavy sadness and hopelessness and couldn't understand why this incident triggered such a strong response in her.

I encouraged her to talk of her own childhood, and she remembered that she too had been a very exuberant child—full of healthy vitality and an urge "to skip, run, and hop." But she remembered having "to sit on it all" because her home was oppressive and her parents viewed exuberance as lack of control, wildness, and potentially dangerous. She went on to describe the oppressive, depressed, and "generally heavy" atmosphere that pervaded her early childhood, and wept very heavily in recalling her sense of chronic misery and frustration. She then realized that her current feelings were exactly those she had felt as a young child in her mother's home, and that the resurgence of that mood and those feelings began right after she "dragged her daughter into the house." She went on to describe her hopelessness because here she was "perpetuating the whole thing, because now I'm doing it to my daughter just as my mother did it to me." I pointed out that there is a major difference. Her mother had not known that she "was doing it," and she does know, making choice and change possible. She said that she felt "so guilty." I cautioned her that guilt played no constructive role in change; on the contrary, by depleting us of energy and a strong sense of self, guilt makes change more difficult. I asked her if she remembered ever running out in the rain as a child. She said that she wasn't sure she did exactly that but she is sure she would have liked to do it many times and could understand how her little girl felt. I asked her what she would have liked her mother to do had she run out to play in the cold rain. She answered, "I would have liked my mother to run out and to play with me for a while—not long, even just for a few minutes—and then to have given me a hot bath, rubbed me down red with a big towel, and then for both of us to have had hot chocolate with marshmallows floating in it." She smiled and said that maybe that's just what she would do the next time her daughter gave her the chance.

. . .

MY FATHER used to get terrible attacks of restlessness and wanderlust. When these hit him he could hardly wait to drop everything and to take off. Sometimes it was only for a few hours, other times it was for several weeks. I went along a few times but mostly he went himself. He'd get into a car (he always owned a secondhand car which invariably needed "work") and ride into the "country" because most of the time his urge involved "seeing mountains and breathing some mountain air." He wanted my mother to go along with him, but this was the one issue in which she did assert herself and with absolute finality. She in no way stood in his way or attempted to discourage his going, but she preferred to stay at home and at home she stayed.

But he managed to get into a fight with all of us with unfailing regularity before he left each time. I say "fight," and yet it wasn't a real fight at all because a fight requires antagonists and we were not antagonistic to him either before, during, or after his trips. The "fights" were contrivances purely of his own invention, and our role during them was to provide a kind of sounding board for his projections because the entire scene was invented and embroidered by him. He would start with some minor irritation, work it up and blow it up to larger but very thin proportions, and sustain it until he left in what seemed like an angry mood and which in some way suggested that this escape was necessary because he had been somehow put upon by us. Perhaps in a way he did feel "put upon," but if so it had nothing at all to do with the immediate time before each departure. Perhaps he was put upon in terms of the responsibility we, his family, represented and the boredom he often suffered making that all-important but burdensome and necessary "living," because my father was in large part a gypsy, a poet, and I think a frustrated scholar.

Moving from home to home and these short trips away from whatever current situation we were living in provided his only outlet. But these voyage-prelude tirades (and looking back now I realize none of us were ever in the least disturbed by them) served other purposes. They assuaged his guilt, making it possible for him to indulge his need by rationalizing our not understanding him as a reason for leaving—one of the common complaints he had in these "fights." He also needed these fights to break his ties to home. And as much of a gypsy as he was, whichever current place we lived in was home because we, his family, were his security blanket and represented much of his self-identifying roots.

So there he was, deeply mixed in a very common conflict, dependent on us for a sense of identification and security, and pressured by us in the responsibility we represented. On the one hand he needed us, and on the other we represented lack of freedom largely thwarted by his dependency on us as well as the need to "make a living" we produced. Those periodic escapes were a necessary supplement to another scenario I have described earlier, in which my mother asked where he was going each time he went outside and he said that he did not have to tell her, all this to give some small credence to his need for "being free." The "prelude fights" were necessary to temporarily break the bond so that he could take off for a short while. We got to understand this, my mother, sister, Ellie, and eventually my children too, because this went on well into his seventies. We knew exactly when a trip was forthcoming because we always recognized the contrived fight and had no difficulty at all differentiating it from "real fights." But he didn't know, and we never told him. We just went along, mostly passively but sometimes helping him along by providing a "little irritation." Telling him would have spoiled it for him. It would have made it harder to take the trips and probably would have made him feel foolish attempting to generate synthetic fights once he knew about them consciously. We never discussed not telling him, but we somehow, perhaps unconsciously, silently and mutually agreed not to tell him and to go along with his exercise.

IN MY FATHER'S LAST YEARS a change took place. These contrived fights stopped, as did his trips away from home. He also stopped moving and lived in the same place for more than ten years. "Real fights" stopped too. I don't think he became "resigned" or "settled into old age"—waiting for death or anything like that. On the contrary, his mind was clear and lively and extremely perceptive and tuned into everything, everybody, and the world around him generally, more than ever before. In fact he had always been extremely intelligent, but in old age he became very wise. His perspectives and outlook generally made it fulfilling, soothing, and enriching to be and to talk with him, something that would have seemed impossible years earlier. This sounds like the old line in which the son says, "Gee, dad, you finally got very smart," when of course it was the son who finally grew up. This is also partly the case. I think we both got over considerable sick pride and narcissism which made cooperative communication between us so difficult. Yet I believe now that even in those years during which we could not talk to each other without fighting, even then, during verbal fights a great deal of warmth and even mutual compassion and understanding passed between us on a deeper, feeling level. Because surely in each other we viewed our own inner conflicts and frustrations, we were so much alike. But in later years our words changed and I suspect became one with our feelings. Dissolution of sick pride and the need to fulfill sick self-image values in ourselves made it possible. My father was no longer the despot and had found a new or perhaps a very old humility, and he was even able to accept various dependencies on me with equanimity. Those last years were not unlike our earliest ones and there was much openness, tenderness, and intimacy that passed between us.

SOMETHING "FUNNY" HAPPENED this afternoon. I was walking home from downtown on Madison Avenue, wondering why the fancy stores and boutiques never spread from the uptown area. I suddenly realized that I'd never make it back in time for an appointment I had with a patient if I continued walking. I decided to take a taxi and waited on the corner of Thirtieth and Madison, but for ten minutes I saw no taxi. I was about to give up and start walking again when two things happened simultaneously. A taxi came into sight about six blocks downtown, having probably cut into Madison from Fifth Avenue, and a disconnected thought popped into my mind (consciousness). The thought was "much ado about nothing." It had nothing at all to do with what I had been thinking about earlier and consciously seemed in no way connected to any feeling, thought, or activity I was involved in. These kinds of intrusive or seemingly disconnected thoughts sometimes occur in all of us, and I suspect for the most part we ignore and thus deny them because it can be quite disconcerting to realize that seemingly illogical, disconnected, inappropriate stuff over which we have no control can come up from the inner depths. In short, any sudden confrontation with the unconscious can be frightening. But if we don't deny by casting aside, but rather pursue with associations that come relative to that thought, feeling, or fantasy, we often find out that the "intruder" is not disconnected at all. It almost always connects to some well of inner feelings we are attempting to keep out of awareness and which at the same time we are trying to become aware of. The whole psychoanalytic process is based on just this kind of free associative activity, and leads to rather remarkable and helpful insights as consciousness of what we really feel and who we are is extended. So I attempted to pursue the thought as the taxi slowly approached, but to no avail. I had no associations relative to the thought "much ado about nothing," and no connected feelings to it either. I am well aware of the kind of resistance we sometimes have to awareness, and as I waved the taxi to a stop I thought this was one of those times. My mind was blank.

I sat down in the cab and told the driver where I wanted to go. We almost immediately got into a little traffic and had to stop for a few minutes. The driver turned around to me and said, "I look like just another cab driver, I suppose." Before I could think of an answer I thought, *here is still another philosopher taxi driver*. He went on, "There's one big difference. Tell me, how many cab drivers have you known whose biggest interest in Shakespeare?" "None," I admitted. He went on to tell me that he saved his money and traveled all over the country, and to England once too, to attend Shakespeare festivals. I said nothing and just listened attentively, but I sensed that something was coming that would click in place—just what I didn't yet know. He told me that he was fifty-eight years old and that Shakespeare had been a "passion" with him since he was old enough to reason, to listen, and to read. And then he told me that even though he "might seem shallow"—and now I had a sense of acute anticipation, but still no inkling—"the comedies appealed" to him more than the tragedies, though he "certainly appreciated the greatness of the tragedies." And then he said it, and I felt that kind of inner click in place, "My favorite work is *Much Ado About Nothing*. I've seen it any number of times and will probably go on seeing it again and again." We arrived at Sixty-second and Third, the corner of my street, and

I paid the fare and left saying something kind of inane like "keep enjoying yourself," or something like that.

After I arrived home I recalled a few other "uncanny" incidents (I heard someone call these kinds of experiences "uncanny," and it's probably as good a term as any, though the term "inexplicable" is pretty good too).

At the time that Ellie had just become pregnant with Eugene I saw a man in several consultations who suffered from chronic depression. I advised him of the treatment he needed, referred him to an appropriate therapist, and after those few sessions did not see him again. During our second session he told me of a dream he had the night before our meeting. He dreamed that there was a room in the house I lived in (I lived in Brooklyn at the time), and he described the location of the room and its contents in detail, including a crib with a baby boy in it. He described the baby in detail. I thought of many dreams of this kind I had heard before which sometimes alluded to the new sense of self (rebirth) a patient seeks in coming into treatment. But of course I also thought of the fact that Ellie was pregnant. The man did not know that, had never met Ellie, and knew nothing of the arrangements of the house I lived in. After Ellie gave birth to Eugene I realized that the man had in his dream described Eugene and his room in the house with absolute accuracy down to the most minute detail—his complexion, hair, eye color, temperament (he was very lively and loud), as well as every bit of furniture and its arrangement in the room, including a detailed description of the crib. Ellie had arranged the room and bought the crib and other things, including a small rocker which she used and which my patient's dream described.

There was another patient whom I had in treatment for several years whose free associations often exactly matched my own. It was *almost* as if we read each other's minds (which I don't believe), often saying the same things at exactly the same time or having the same thought at the same time. For example, on one occasion he could not remember the name of a proctologist whom he wanted to tell me about. We both blurted out a name at the same time, which was not the name of the proctologist at all and sounded nothing like it but was rather the name of a cardiologist. I suppose our associative tracts were much alike and not being able to think of one specialist's name, we thought of another whom we both happened to know. But we did not have similar backgrounds at all, nor was our general frame of reference or use of symbols and language particularly alike. As a matter of fact we generally had very little in common except the experience of very frequently having the same association. Both he and I often said "I know what you are thinking," and very often we'd prove to be right.

Ellie and I had another "uncanny experience."

Like all good and true New York psychoanalysts I always took my vacations during the month of August. Also like a great many New York analysts, for ten years we rented a house for the month on Cape Cod—more specifically in South Truro. How this tradition of time and place got started nobody seems to know, but as I think Woody Allen once said, "God forbid anyone in New York needs psychiatric help in August." It is interesting that members of the various schools of psychoanalysis do not get along well together and that there is no easy and constructive exchange of worthwhile professional information between these professional "human communication helpers." But this does not pertain to choice of vacation time, and at least to some extent to place, too, because in this regard we are almost religiously in accord. I suppose it is an ancient tradition perhaps established by Freud himself, and few of us dare veer from it.

A lawyer, let's call him Mr. Lawyer, owned a house across

the road from the one we rented in South Truro. We were on a "hello" basis with Mr. and Mrs. Lawyer and nothing more; we never met socially or even on the beach.

One day shortly after we bought a house on Ninety-third Street and Fifth Avenue some years ago we bumped into Mr. and Mrs. Lawyer in the street and again exchanged our usual "hellos." He asked where we lived and we told him. He told us that they just moved out of the house next door. I didn't ask where their new home was. Several years later, a few days after moving to an apartment at 180 East End Avenue, a beautiful street overlooking Carl Schurz Park and the East River, we again bumped into the Lawyers and again exchanged "hellos" and told Mr. Lawyer where we had just moved. It turned out that they had just moved out of 180 East End Avenue. A number of years went by and we decided to try living in the area near Westport, Connecticut, to fight our addiction to New York (it did not work and we soon moved back) and to give up the city ("the city" is of course a New York chauvinistic term, and by "the city" New Yorkers only mean New York City, no matter whether they are in London or Hong Kong when they—we—use the term). We searched for more than a year and finally found a house we liked in Weston. We bought it and then at one point, after we had lived there a short while, we happened to come across the building plans of the house which informed us in letters across the top of the plans that the builders and original owners of the house were our "hello friends," the Lawyers.

So what about "uncanny experiences"? I'm sure all of us have had them and many of us would like to believe that they are really more mysterious, magical, mystical, powerful, than they are. And then there are people like myself who have always believed that much and maybe all can be explained on the basis of coincidence, however much huge odds may be involved in particular instances. And I'm well aware of the powerful "vested interest" I've had in fighting all notions such as ESP, supernatural forces, and the like, and absolutely insisting on logical and rational explanations which eventually have the potential to be scientifically validated. Perhaps my own feelings about these matters are a function of my own security needs, which are based in large part on intellectual rationale and logic, and which would be shaken by any kind of credence to the so-called occult or extra-sensory perception. I apologize for lumping the latter together because I am aware that there are serious researchers who do believe in ESP; I suppose my doing this is further evidence of my prejudice and perhaps also my fear.

In talking about these matters my older son, who is also a psychiatrist and analyst, and who has been more of a scholar than I, says that Jung feels that these experiences just are what they are and require no explanation. But this is very difficult for people who don't have the dedication to the spiritual characteristic of Carl Gustav Jung and who as a matter of fact have been just as religiously trained to be pragmatic and to need to understand with logic. Yet when these "magic" things occur, if they are not accepted as such—as just being there—they tend to clash with the need for rationale and do produce at least some uneasiness. Theoretical explanations and contrived theories do not make the reverberations of uneasiness go away. I suppose those people who "have faith" in humans having powers or senses which are more than human, or in ESP phenomena, or in superhuman forces—and again I've lumped too much together—do not suffer these jolts to their logical order of things. On the contrary, they probably not only regard these phenomena with interest but accept them with the joy that comes when faith is once again endorsed and relived.

But despite myself and my repeated attempts, and even struggle, to be more open to "other kinds of explanations," such as perhaps the non-explanation of Jung (just feeling it and accepting), I don't seem to succeed. My mind goes to thoughts of coincidence, taste, values, goals, and desires some of us have in common which produce similar or same experiences; enormous powers of perception which we do have, so that we perceive and register much we are not consciously aware we perceive, and communicate much of this, without awareness, to our fellows, too. I may have in some way told my patient of my wife's pregnancy without either of us being aware that I had. But how did he predict how Eugene would look and the arrangement of the furniture? Did I perhaps see a poster that advertised *Much Ado About Nothing* without realizing it? But what of the remarkable coincidence of the cab driver? Did he see it too? I did "pick" a cab driver who was obsessed with Shakespeare and did in fact know a great deal about him. But, but, but, there's obviously much that goes on in and between us which defies quick or even slow explanation. I am also sure that just as there is much more that goes on in each of us on an unconscious level than on a conscious level, the same also applies to that which goes on between any of us. But it is very hard to be open to *other ways* of viewing or feeling *other kinds* or all kinds of experiences, human experiences.

THERE IS a very small Greek "shopping center" which establishes itself every morning on our corner, Sixty-second Street and Third Avenue. The woman and her bouquets of flowers are dropped off at the phone booth on the corner by a man (I presume her husband) every morning at seven-thirty, and her makeshift stand is arranged a few feet from the booth on Third Avenue by eight-thirty, just about when people begin to pass to go to work. She stands or sits on a little wooden box all day, and there she eats the lunch which she brings with her. This consists of cheese, a sandwich, fruit, and coffee. She is in her early thirties, has a beautiful face, high cheek-bones, brown eyes, thick brown hair, smooth skin, rosy com-plexion, and is of medium height—a bit on the heavy side. She looks earthy and strong. Her son, who is about nine years old, comes to help her at three-thirty (after school) and looks almost exactly like his mother. He speaks to her in Greek, and usually spends about an hour playing ball with a fragile-looking boy about his age who lives in a luxury apartment house on Sixty-second Street, two buildings from the corner. The boy speaks English, and her son speaks without any accent. At seven o'clock in the evening the man arrives in the small pickup to take them home. By that time she is usually sold out. Ellie, who loves flowers, is probably her best customer.

A Greek man, in his late forties, also strong looking, dark, of medium height, arrives at nine o'clock each morning with his push stand hot dog cart. His large umbrella and business is set up in ten minutes. He sells boiled frankfurters in rolls and large spicy sausages with either hot onions or sauerkraut and all kinds of flavored sodas. He sets his stand up on Sixty-second Street just a few feet from the corner. He and the flower lady meet on the corner and have conversations in Greek several times a day. Now and then her son joins in too. She, her husband, her son, and the hot dog man talk for at least a few minutes each night before she leaves. The hot dog man doesn't leave until seven in the evening. My son Eugene is surely his best customer and eats many hot dogs and sausages between meals. When there is no business, the flower lady usually sits on her wooden box and seems to be daydreaming. The hot dog man does not sit; from the time he arrives until he leaves, he stands and waits for business. Occasionally they watch each others' places while I presume one goes off to the bathroom, probably at Bloomingdale's or one of the local restaurants. On Saturdays the flower lady's son is there with his mother all day and usually spends several hours playing with the fragile-looking boy from the apartment house. They are not there on Sundays. This routine does not vary and I've yet to see them miss a day, winter or summer. When it rains, the hot dog man huddles under his umbrella and the flower lady stands either in the phone booth or in one of the store entrances. There is a large and very fancy optometry shop on the corner. I've talked to the hot dog man a few times and greet him each time I pass the corner. He speaks English with some difficulty but enough to indicate that he is very bright and has a quick sense of humor. I've bought some flowers now and then, and greet the woman sometimes when I pass, and my impression is that she speaks no English at all. Her son seems very busy all the time, either in discussions with his mother or the hot dog man or playing ball or standing and daydreaming, and so I haven't talked to him at all.

It's the son I wonder about, and I'm sure I identify with him. It's not at all hard for me to recall helping my father in the store at the beach and operating a little ice cream stand on the corner and selling mello rolls and root beer. There were times I felt put upon and wanted to go out and play, full-time. There were times I envied "rich kids" whose parents were born in this country and even whose parents' parents were born here, because everything seemed to me to be so much "safer" for them, so much more secure and predictable. And *now* I would not have had it different, not any of it; I would not trade one second of it, not even the worries my parents had when it rained and business was bad. I remember how ecstatic they felt when it was hot and sunny and they knew crowds of people would come to the beach so that plenty of ice cream, sodas, suntan lotion, and other sundries would be sold. I remember counting dollars and silver with them one late night at the end of what must have been the hottest and busiest day in twenty-five years at the beach. The total came to one hundred twenty-three dollars, and we felt rich beyond belief and celebrated by eating big turkey sandwiches on seeded rolls with Russian dressing, all bought in a local Greek restaurant, the owners of which struggled and were sad and happy with weather and business fluctuations as we were. I remember being twelve years old and the pride I felt in my father's confidence in me when I carried a brown bag full of money to the bank, alone, taking several buses to get there. I always feel a closeness to small storekeepers of all kinds, and I always remember the kind of closeness and warmth that comes of everyone helping and sharing in the business together. How different this must be from having a father who goes off in the morning and isn't seen again until that night. And so I look at the flower lady's son and for some reason picture old men eating mello roll ice cream cones walking in the street, and it gives me a warm feeling, and I go on to wonder how he will feel about this time in his life many years from now. Of course he will remember.

A PATIENT OF MINE had to go out of town for several months a few weeks ago. She felt quite anxious about interrupting her treatment and suggested we hold our sessions on the phone. I acquiesced, and this is the first time I've had this experience. I should have known better, because I've always used the phone as a means of delivering a quick message rather than a way of engaging in a prolonged conversation; I've never cared to talk on it.

From her point of view the sessions have gone unusually well. She has in fact been more open and productive in revealing herself to both me and to herself, and she has had much richer (more emotionally laden) and pertinent associations on the phone than in our in-person sessions.

For me it's been another story entirely. The session starts out all right, and then about halfway through I start to feel nauseous and restless and it takes much effort and all my determination to stay with it. I thought that perhaps part of my reaction had a physical basis. Since we are used to listening to sound with both ears, perhaps listening with one ear produces an imbalance leading to nausea. On the basis of this theory and my love for gadgets (I suppose these reasons should be reversed on the basis of relative importance) I bought a machine which permits listening without the phone and with both ears. It has helped considerably: the nausea has gone away. But the restlessness and the struggle to concentrate continue. I believe that at best communication by phone is limited. Seeing each other and feeling each other's presence and perceiving and registering all of the nuances expressed by hand, face, and body gestures and expressions convey much more than disembodied telephone voices.

But obviously my strong feelings in this matter indicate a bias which goes beyond these objective realities.

I think that it really comes down to the differences in my patient's and my own character structures. She is a reserved, very detached person, and I'm a person of relatively little reserve and on the expansive side, though I do get periodic showers of introspective self-analyzing attacks.

For her the telephone is a distance-making machine which dilutes contact with people enough to make her comfortable. She communicates her feelings better in this way. For me the phone has exactly the reverse effect. Its capacity for distance making dilutes the full contact with people I need in order to communicate fully.

·   ·   ·

I WENT TO BUY SOME CLOTHES today, and in the store—I suppose largely due to the influence of writing this book—I suddenly felt transported way back to when I was about fourteen years old. I remember my father taking me to a store, it may have been Howard's, and buying for me a grey herringbone tweed suit with a vest and two pairs of pants, and a long brown herringbone topcoat, sort of a light winter coat. The whole bill came to $45.50, and my father started an account there so that he could pay it out, I think at the rate of five dollars a month. The completion of forms, checking his identity, making phone calls to the credit department, and so forth took more than an hour. How things have changed. Everything costs so much more now. It's so easy to pay, and it has so little meaning, nothing ceremonial about it at all.

A few days ago my patient, a sensitive, poetic, exceptionally intelligent woman in her mid-forties asked herself about "treats." "Whatever happened to treats? Where have they gone? I don't even hear the word anymore." She recalled, and made me recall to, how when homework was done she went out into the street to play and that was a treat. Both of us remembered ice cream pops and "eating out." I remembered my father taking all of us to see a movie, *Cimarron* with Richard Dix, and then eating in Hechter's Cafeteria. It was a very big occasion in celebration of something, I don't remember what anymore. But I do remember the movie and what we ate in the cafeteria, and the mood of high exhilaration and appreciation we all shared vividly. Whatever did happen to treats? How did everything become so commonplace? How did we come to the point where so much is just taken for granted? Has our culture, our society, changed so much? Does newfound affluence, even moderate affluence, immediately bring on this kind of loss of in-touch, sustained aliveness, a kind of deadening? Is this then the price we pay for "success," a kind of unwitting resignation we slip into and

a flattening of emotional response as regards life's real "treats"? Is there a price to pay for everything after all?

If it isn't the age we live in, is it the age we who live long enough eventually arrive at, middle age? Perhaps the best years are those of struggle, times of heightened contrasts, appreciation of "small things," without the need for excess stimulation. Perhaps there are those of us who are especially blessed by the experience of mutual struggle and the kind of family closeness and coziness which evolves right there in the hardest of times, in the mutual struggle to survive. Is a "treatless world" or a world relatively without treats the price we pay for increased dollar ease and even leisure? Does it have to be this way, or can it be different perhaps even in a dollar world, if we could somehow resist the pressures of sick pride, the need for competitive success, the creation of all kinds of false hierarchies and separation of people from each other, and vindictive triumph, and instead sustain some semblance of compassion for ourselves and each other.

As my patient spoke I had other associations too, other kinds of "treats." But they were more than that, they were evidence of love from someone else and the foundation of real love for self which is most sustaining of everything all of our lives. I remember my mother's enormous capacity for love and acceptance in those early days, the long talks we had, the exchange of feelings and ideas, the countless "little things" she saved up to buy me—socks, gloves, clay sets when I was ill, the Siamese fighting fish which I desperately wanted during a big "tropical fish phase." I remember the excitement over my first secondhand bike. Of course I will always remember the watch. I remember my father helping me build a small sailboat and my mother and sister, both of whom were very skillful, helping me or rather making for me a model airplane.

My patient and I recalled a kind of dedication to fun,

surprises, lolling, strolling, and easygoingness. These things seem so hard to find in this city. Whatever happened to the Duggans man and his cupcakes? Or are they still here? Maybe it's only we who have changed, and for other kids there are still treats and their Duggans man.

MY MOTHER CALLED a short time ago. She said that she had decided to see an analyst. She said that she hoped that it wasn't a great foolishness, because she is eighty-one years old. I assured her that age had nothing at all to do with it—that she is already changing and growing, her decision to get help proves it. She seemed open and responsive. I must find her a therapist immediately—someone who is mainly a loving human being.